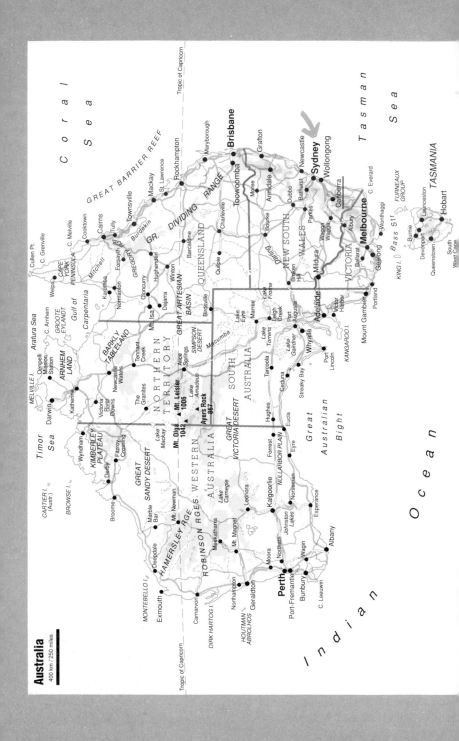

Australia

400 km / 250 miles

Tropic of Capricorn

Tropic of Capricorn

Coral Sea

GREAT BARRIER REEF

CAPE YORK PENINSULA

Cullen Pt.
C. Grenville
Weipa
C. Melville
Cooktown
Cairns
Tully
Townsville
Mackay
St. Lawrence
Rockhampton
Maryborough

Brisbane
Toowoomba
Grafton
Newcastle
Sydney
Wollongong

T a s m a n   S e a

C. Everard

TASMANIA
FURNEAUX GROUP
Launceston
Hobart
Burnie
Devonport
Queenstown
South West Cape

Bass St
KING I.

QUEENSLAND
GR. DIVIDING RANGE
GREGORY RGE
Michell
Karumba
Normanton
Cloncurry
Mt Isa
Hughenden
Winton
Barcaldine
Charleville
Quilpie
Birdsville

Moree
Armidale
Dubbo
Bathurst
Parkes
Canberra
Albury
Wagga Wagga
Bourke
Emden

NEW SOUTH WALES
Darling
Broken Hill
Mildura
VICTORIA
Ballarat
Geelong
Melbourne
Wonthaggi
Portland

Gulf of Carpentaria
Arafura Sea
MELVILLE I.
Oenpelli Mission Station
C. Arnhem
GROOTE EYLANDT
ARNHEM LAND
Darwin
Katherine
Victoria River Downs
Newcastle Waters
Tennant Creek
The Granites

NORTHERN TERRITORY
BARKLY TABLELAND
Alice Springs
Lake Amadeus
▲ Mt. Leisler 1006
Ayers Rock 867
Mt. Olga 1044 ▲
SIMPSON DESERT
GREAT ARTESIAN BASIN
Macumba
Lake Eyre
Marree
Lake Frome
Leigh Creek
Lake Torrens
Lake Gairdner
Port Augusta
Whyalla
Port Pirie
Adelaide
Victor Harbor
Mount Gambier
KANGAROO I.

SOUTH AUSTRALIA
GREAT VICTORIA DESERT
Lake Mackay
Lake Carnegie

WESTERN AUSTRALIA
ROBINSON RGES.
HAMERSLEY RGE.
Marble Bar
Mt. Newman
Meekatharra
Mt. Magnet
Leonora
Kalgoorlie
Norseman
NULLARBOR PLAIN
Forrest
Hughes
Eucla
Cook
Ceduna
Streaky Bay
Port Lincoln
Eyre
Tarcoola

Great Australian Bight

Esperance
Albany
Wagin
Bunbury
C. Leeuwin
Bunbury
Northam
Moora
Johnston Lakes
Perth
Port-Fremantle
Northampton
Geraldton
HOUTMAN ABROLHOS
DIRK HARTOG I.
Carnarvon
Exmouth
MONTEBELLO I.

Indian Ocean

Deepdale
BROWSE I.
Broome
Derby
Fitzroy Crossing
Wyndham
KIMBERLEY PLATEAU
GREAT SANDY DESERT
CARTIER I. (Aust.)

Timor Sea

G'DAY!

Imagine you have friends in Sydney. They have spent years exploring Sydney to discover the best experiences, sightseeing, dining and shopping this exciting city has to offer. As locals, they have gone far beyond regular tourist itineraries, travelling by ferry, car and foot to find the real Sydney.

The local knowledge these friends pass on to you is both personal and opinionated. They guide you to the very heart of what makes Sydney special. They show you where to go and what to do to experience Sydney at its best.

Your guides, David McGonigal and John Borthwick, have lived and worked in Sydney throughout their lives. They are APA's team Down Under and have previously edited APA's *Insight City Guide: Sydney* as well as *Insight Guides* to Australia and the Great Barrier Reef. Despite lengthy sojourns throughout the world, John and David always end up living back in Sydney. As travel writers, photographers and commentators they are experts whose recommended itineraries are based on up-to-the-moment information.

This book is intended for the traveller who wants to savour Sydney, extracting the best from a short stay. It begins with a brief overview of Sydney's quirky history and then leads into a series of easy-to-follow itineraries. These are divided into day tours that give you a good look at the city; several half-day tours of special interest; shopping, nightlife and dining hints; and some excursions beyond the city limits. All the practical information you need – visas, accommodation, services and so on – is in the last section of the book.

While these travel agendas have been carefully planned to take in Sydney's highlights, they are not cast in stone – you should vary them to suit your plans, or merely at whim. Travel is not meant to be a matter of crossing things off a "been there, done that" list. Sydney in particular is a destination that rewards the adventurous.

G' Day! Welcome!

1

Insight Pocket Guide:

SYDNEY

First Edition

© **1992 APA Publications (HK) Ltd.**

All Rights Reserved

Printed in Singapore by

Höfer Press (Pte) Ltd

Fax: 65-861 6438

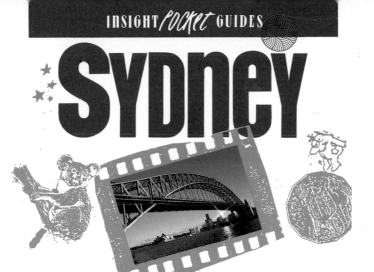

INSIGHT *Pocket* GUIDES
Sydney

Written and Photographed by **David McGonigal and John Borthwick**

Directed by **Hans Höfer**

Design Concept by **V. Barl**

Art Direction by **Karen Hoisington**

INSIGHT
Pocket
GUIDES

Contents

Maps

7

Left, David McGonigal and right, John Borthwick

Dear Reader!

I ran away from Sydney and Australia in 1976. My escape ended four years later when I brought my new Canadian wife back for a three-week holiday. That was well over a decade ago and we're still here. Our downfall was a short ferry trip from Circular Quay to Neutral Bay. As we passed the Opera House and the Harbour Bridge, the sandstone nooks and crannies of the north shore came into view.

In the face of such beauty, "Let's stay longer" was a mutual, instant decision. The love affair with this warm and wonderful harbourside city continues. Still, we are not alone. When British Airways offered free trips on all its routes throughout the world in mid 1991, by far the most popular destination was Sydney. And why not? Few would contest its claim to being one of the world's most scenically spectacular cities, a shimmering delight of sunlight off water and golden beaches.

But Sydney is not a sanitised rendition of the Emerald City of Oz. Rather, it's fairly clean, relatively unpolluted and reasonably safe – but its streets are by no means paved with gold. Instead, they are littered with parking police and dreams that, while not broken, are often askew. But the real joy of Sydney is that only a few minutes beyond the concrete chasms of the Central Business District is Circular Quay and a tranquil ferry trip to Manly.

In the 1990s Sydney no longer feels like the City at the End of the Universe, a sleepy place where work merely filled the day until it was cool enough to go to the beach. It has a new vibrancy, but the harbour and beaches remain the feature that make Sydney special. As I found, after a sunny summer day on the water with a few cold beers, it can be a place that is very hard to leave.

It's a great place to live and visit, but a lot of guff has been spoken about Sydney being "the best address on earth". In reality the best address on earth is probably just "home" – wherever one's mountain, molehill or *motu* might be. Nevertheless, that home *and* Sydney are for me the same place is something I would count as a definite blessing.

A childhood spent by this Pacific city's coves, bushlands and booming surf has rather ruined me for a life in other higher and higher rising metropolises where "the great outdoors" is a pot plant on a 27th-floor balcony and "freedom" might be a choice of 12 poodle-clipping services. And so it is to Sydney that I return time and again to replenish my sanity and coffers.

This is not the return of the parochial chauvinist but of the appreciative son who loves the eccentricities of the place. Like the harbour ferries in their weekend lassitude or peak-hour pushiness, the inefficiency of half the population and the good cheer of the other half, the month-long sweaty siesta of January, the roaring forty thousand at a State of Origin winter football game, and the temperings of our Anglo-European assumptions by the ever-growing Asianisation of the place.

I like to show friends around Sydney, because in doing so I rediscover the place I call home. Excavating the city's sights and frights again from the encrustations of my habits and too-familiar perceptions, I feel refreshed by this new role, of being a tourist at home. I hope some of this pleasure in rediscovery and "un-covery" comes through in these journeys which we are about to take together.

John Borthwick

HISTORY

Sydney is one of the world's oldest *and* newest cities. It is estimated that the first inhabitants arrived here some 50,000 years ago. However, despite the development of an intricate social fabric, those early Aborigines imposed little change – and certainly no damage – on the landscape. All that changed a little over 200 years ago when the British Government decided to locate an open-air gaol here. Since then Sydney has grown to fill much of the available land between the sea and the Blue Mountains.

Beginnings: When the first Aborigines came to what is now Sydney the harbour did not exist: it was a dry valley about 10 kilometres (six miles) inland. The earliest stone tools found in the region date back more than 45,000 years. About 10,000 years ago the ice caps started to melt and coastlines altered until the seas stabilised at their present level, about 6,000 years before Europeans arrived.

Captain Cook did not discover Australia. By 29 April 1770, when the 41-year-old British Royal Navy officer sailed the *Endeavour* into a sheltered bay where he noted a "fine meadow", the north, south and west coasts of the continent had already been explored by Dutch, Portuguese and Spanish navigators over the previous two centuries. But none had ventured as far as the east coast, which Cook followed from about the present New South Wales-Victorian border to Botany

"The finest harbour in the world"

CAPTAIN COOK
LANDED HERE
28TH APRIL. A.D. 1770.
THIS MONUMENT
WAS ERECTED A.D. 1870,
BY THE HONORABLE THOMAS HOLT, M.L.C
VICTORIA REGINA.THE EARL OF BELMORE.GOVERNOR &c

Kurnell – where Cook first stepped ashore.

Bay and upwards to the tip of Queensland at Cape York.

The *Endeavour* spent a week in Botany Bay but the crew had little contact with the 3,000 local Aborigines. Cook noted that "All they seemed to want was for us to be gone."

At first the English government had little use for the land which Cook had claimed in the name of the crown. However, the American Declaration of Independence in 1776 stopped transportation of convicts to the southern plantations and penal settlements such as Georgia. With that door closed, English gaols soon filled and rotting hulks of ships on the Thames River took the overflow. In August 1786, Lord Sydney (Thomas Townsend), the British Home Secretary, instructed the Admiralty to arrange for Botany Bay to receive a fleet of marines and convicts. It was the inauspicious start of a new nation.

First Settlement: On 13 May 1787 a fleet of 11 ships sailed from Portsmouth, and laboured into Botany Bay, 22,500 kilometres (14,000 miles) away on 20 January 1788. An inadequate water supply there led Captain-General Arthur Phillip into Port Jackson (which James Cook had merely noted in passing) and found what he declared to be "the finest harbour in the world". The whole colony moved to "Sydney Cove". On Saturday 26 January 1788, the Union Jack flew for the first time over the tiny settlement of 568 male and 191 female convicts, plus 200 marines accompanied by 27 wives and 25 children.

Captain Cook

There was every likelihood during those first years that the colony would starve and founder. The Aborigines kept away, so the settlers had to find out for themselves how to survive in a land far different from any they knew. By mid-1790 the colony was saved from starvation only

Old Sydney Town – historical repeats

when a supply ship arrived. Soon afterwards the Second Fleet came into port in terrible condition: 267 convicts had died on the voyage and a further 124 died soon after their arrival.

The settlers clung to the foreshores of Sydney Cove for a long time. Governor Phillip devised a town plan but everyone ignored it, bringing about the haphazard street grid of present-day Sydney. Phillip was followed by governors Hunter, King and then Bligh. The last came to Sydney on his first appointment after the mutiny on the *Bounty*.

Beginnings of Nationhood: The inspired 12-year term of Governor Lachlan Macquarie from 1810 to 1821 took New South Wales from foundling colony to fledgling community. Sydney continues to bears the indelible stamp of Macquarie and his principal architect, the forger, convict and genius Francis Greenway. It was Macquarie who established a designated street width (with footpaths) and demolished any buildings which stood in its way. Greenway-designed churches that survive today include St James' in the city, St Matthew's at Windsor and St Luke's in Liverpool. Governor Macquarie pardoned Greenway after he designed Hyde Park Barracks (still standing in Macquarie Street), but Greenway's fortunes declined after his patron departed: Commissioner Bigge considered his work "too grand for an infant colony".

Governor Macquarie also gave Australia its name when, in 1817, he first used the word "Australia" in his correspondence. The word came from the earlier expression "*Terra Australis*", meaning simply south land.

Although it took 24 years to find a way across the Blue Mountains to the pasture lands of the west, the population of Sydney increased rapidly when the convict numbers were boosted by the arrival of free settlers. Even so, by 1820 the town of Sydney barely covered a square mile (2.5 square kilometres). The first street in

Australia was the bullock track that became George Street and the first road leading out of Sydney was built to Parramatta in 1794.

Smallpox killed half the Aboriginal population before the colony was two years old and within 50 years of white settlement less than 300 Aborigines remained in the region. Even so, many Sydney suburbs were given Aboriginal names.

Transportation of convicts ceased in 1840. A total of 83,000 convicts had been sent to New South Wales and most stayed here to make a home in the colony. Charles Darwin, later the author of *The Origin of Species*, visited Sydney in 1836 and concluded that: "as a real system of reform it has failed ... but as a means of making men outwardly honest – of converting vagabonds most useless in one hemisphere into active citizens of another, and thus giving birth to a new and splendid country – a grand centre of civilisation – it has succeeded to a degree perhaps unparalleled in history."

Gold Rush: Sydney town was declared the City of Sydney in July 1842. Less than a decade later Australia's first publicised gold discovery was made near Bathurst, on the other side of the Blue Mountains, by E H Hargraves. Hargraves returned from the California gold fields claiming that they had reminded him of parts of New South Wales. Despite general ridicule, he proceeded from Sydney to Bathurst with an acquaintance and announced that they were standing on gold. His first panful of dirt produced gold and he declared: "Here it is. This is memorable day in the history of New South Wales. I shall be a baronet, and you will be knighted, and my old horse will be stuffed, put in a glass case, and sent to the British Museum!" He was right about the gold but wrong about the rest – the remainder of his life was uneventful until he died in 1891.

Hargraves' discovery started a rush that boosted the fortunes of Sydney: its population nearly doubled in 10 years (54,000 in 1851, 96,000 in 1861). The main city streets were paved with wooden blocks by 1885, finally removing the dust pall which had plagued the city. Buildings fitting the image of a city of Victoria's Britain were being built, including the Town Hall (1889), the Customs House (1887), and the Art Gallery, which was begun in the 1880s. In 1895, Samuel Clements (Mark Twain) visited Sydney and declared it "an English city with American trimmings." The same accusation is still made today.

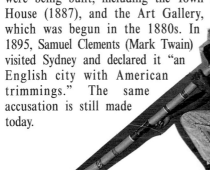

Aboriginal didgeridoo players busking at Circular Quay

Australian Federation: On 1 January 1901 the Commonwealth of Australia came into existence. Thousands of people poured into Centennial Park in Sydney to watch the swearing-in of Australia's first Governor General. By this time, Sydney was a vibrant city with an established literary and arts movement – it had come a long way from the days when life was merely a matter of survival.

However, at this time Sydney was recovering from the major depression of 1892. The Australian colonies largely traded themselves out of trouble by greatly expanding the areas under wheat. A more immediate urban problem was an outbreak of bubonic plague which killed 112 people in Sydney in 1900. The direct result was that the slums of the Rocks had a long overdue clean-up.

In 1909 Australia's first flight took place at Narrabeen Beach where Mr G A Taylor flew a motorless aircraft. Early aviators received heroes' welcomes when they touched down at the field, which was later named Kingsford Smith Airport after Australia's greatest pioneer aviator.

World Wars: On 18 August 1914, the Australian Naval and Military Expeditionary Force left Sydney for German New Guinea, becoming the first Australian troops to join World War 1. During the next four years, 60,000 of the 330,000 Australian troops who served overseas died.

The post-war period was a time of innovation, but this was followed by the Great Depression. The debate on how to tackle the debilitating level of unemployment developed into a class war: the Labor goverment of Premier Jack Lang against the right-wing New Guard. When the Sydney Harbour Bridge was opened in March 1932 Captain de Groot of the paramilitary New Guard slashed the ribbon with his sword before Jack Lang could ceremonially cut it.

In 1921, there were 30,000 cars registered in New South Wales: this figure had risen to more than 625,000 in 1961 and 1.4 million in 1975. A casualty of the reign of the motor car was the Sydney tram. Although the expression "shoot through like a Bondi tram" is still occasionally used, the last tram finished its run in 1961. Not only the automobile population grew dramatically. From half a million at the turn of the century, Sydney's population passed one million before 1931 and two million before 1961. It currently stands at over 3.5 million.

Changing Populations and Attitudes: After World War 2, the stream of new arrivals continued as many left Europe seeking a

Customs House's imperial insignia

Open air jazz

new life for themselves. Over 75 percent of Sydney's population growth between 1947 and 1971 came from immigrants (almost all were from Europe, especially Italy and Greece) and their Australian-born children. This (and subsequent influxes) changed Sydney from a very insular colonial outpost into a multicultural cosmopolitan city.

One of the tallest buildings in Sydney before World War 2 was the 11-storey Australasian Temperance & General Mutual Life Assurance Company building. In 1961, the AMP Insurance Company finished its 26-storey building in Circular Quay. Crowds flocked to marvel at the view from the top of this building. By 1968, the vogue rooftop eyrie was the 50-floor circular tower of Australia Square. The highest construction in Sydney to date – at 1,000 feet (305 metres) – is the Sydney Tower on top of Centrepoint.

From the soul-searching Vietnam moratorium marches of the late 1960s and early 1970s, Sydney appeared to slip into social somnolence during most of the 1970s. There was a moment of fervour in 1975, when Labor prime minister Gough Whitlam was dismissed and people took to the streets in a display of solidarity similar to the one that marked Premier Lang's dismissal – also by the vice-regal representative – over 40 years earlier. But it was short-lived. Instead, the 1970s slipped into the 1980s and the age of the yuppie, when lives became "lifestyles", as profound and as hairstyles fashioned and equally conspicuous.

Sydney woke on 26 January 1988 to greet the dawn of the third century of white settlement. Everyone expected the day to be a great party, and it was all that and more. Despite our best efforts to trivialise it, many Sydneysiders were surprised to find themselves at a turning point in history – the city has come of age.

Milestones

50,000 BC (approximate)**:** Aborigines arrive.

29 April 1770: Captain James Cook sails the *Endeavour* into Botany Bay.

August 1786: Lord Sydney (Thomas Townsend), the Home Secretary, instructs the British Admiralty to arrange what was to be dubbed a "colony of thieves" at Botany Bay.

13 May 1787: A fleet of 11 ships sail from Portsmouth, bound for Botany Bay.

20 January 1788: The First Fleet arrives in Botany Bay.

26 January 1788: The new colony moves to Sydney Cove.

1794: The first road leading out of Sydney is built to Parramatta.

1804: Irish prisoners rise against the government at Vinegar Hill (Rouse Hill).

1810–1821: Governor Lachlan Macquarie takes New South Wales from colony to fledgling community. Sydney's population (1810) is 6,156.

1817: Lachlan Macquarie first uses the word "Australia" in official correspondence.

1820: Sydney's area extends to one square mile (2.5 square kilometres).

1828: Sydney's population is 10,815.

1832: Free settlers are offered assisted passage to the new colony.

1840: Transportation to New South Wales ceases (a total of 83,000 convicts were sent).

July 1842: Sydney town declared the City of Sydney.

1851: The first publicised gold discovery in Australia is made near Bathurst by E H Hargraves.

1861: Sydney's population has doubled in 10 years to reach 96,000.

1890–1891: Serious labour strikes in the colony.

1892: Sydney and the other Australian colonies experience a major depression.

1889: Sydney Town Hall opens.

1900: Outbreak of bubonic plague kills 112. The Rocks has a long overdue cleanup.

1 January 1901: Australian Federation. Australia's first governor general, Lord Hopeton, is sworn in at Centennial Park.

1909: Australia's first aerial flight takes place at Narrabeen Beach.

1912: Australia's first air race between Sydney and Parramatta.

18 August 1914: First Australian troops to join World War 1 leave Sydney for German New Guinea.

1926: Sydney's underground railway opens.

1930: England–Australia Telephone Service commences, putting Sydney in direct voice contact with London.

1931: Sydney's population passes one million.

March 1932: Sydney Harbour Bridge opens.

May 1942: Three Japanese midget submarines enter Sydney Harbour and torpedo a ferry.

1960: Eight-year-old Graham Thorne becomes Australia's first kidnap-ransom victim.

1961: The last Sydney tram finishes its run. The AMP insurance company opens its 26-storey building at Circular Quay.

1966: Australia's currency changes from pounds, shillings and pence to decimal dollars and cents.

1968: The 50-floor circular tower of Australia Square opens.

1973: Sydney Opera House is officially opened by Queen Elizabeth II. Patrick White receives the Nobel Prize for Literature.

1975: Labor Prime Minister Gough Whitlam dismissed amid great controversy.

1979: The long-awaited Eastern Suburbs railway opens.

24 October 1980: Multicultural television station SBS begins transmission in Sydney and Melbourne.

1981: Pat O'Shane, Australia's first Aboriginal law graduate, becomes the first woman to head a New South Wales government department.

29 July 1982: The Australian dollar falls below the value of the US dollar for the first time.

26 January 1988: Celebration of Australia's bicentennary.

1991: North and south tunnels drilled beneath Sydney Harbour meet for a new expressway.

Right, Governor William Bligh surveys Sydney Cove, site of yet another mutiny against him

Day itineraries

Day ①

City Highlights

This might seem like a very full day – but why not try? There's a taste of Sydney Harbour's shores of distant and near history, the shopping-spree Central Business District and good eats in Oxford Street – plus a Kings Cross evening of scarlet libidos.

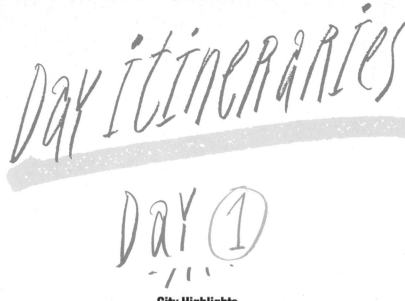

1 Wharf Theatre Restaurant	8 Overseas Passenger Terminal
2 Lord Nelson Hotel	9 Cadmans Cottage
3 Garrison Church	10 Circular Quay
4 Argyle Arts Centre	11 Park Hyatt Hotel
5 Clocktower Centre	12 Hero of Waterloo
6 Pier One	13 Museum of Contemporary Art
7 Earth Exchange	14 Opera House
	15 Customs House
	16 Glasshouse Pyramid
	17 Nikko Hotel

City Highlights
800 m / 0.5 miles

18 Skygarden	
19 Sydney Tower	
20 Queen Victoria Bldg.	
21 Burdekin Hotel	
22 Albury Hotel	
23 Acad. Twin Cinema	
24 Town Hall	
25 Strand Arcade	

To meet Sydney on its own terms, do it early, say by 8 or 9 am. First slip on some good walking shoes, then hail a taxi – for **"Mrs Macquarie's Point"** at the end of **Art Gallery Road**. The view affords a fine profile of the Opera House, tiny **Pinchgut Island**, the north side of the harbour and the Japanese honeymooners frequently photographed here. Overlook the threadbare "ex-lawn" and have a chuckle at the queue of tour groups (the reason for the lawn's demise) posing before that operatic backdrop.

It's a short walk around **Farm Cove** (so named because this was the site of the first European farm on the continent) to the Opera

18

Sydney Opera House, Bennelong Point

House along the shoreline path which skirts the **Royal Botanic Gardens** (tel: 2318111). Wander through the pretty 30 hectares (74 acres) of duck ponds, statues, Australian flora and imported exotics, and check out the tropical plants in the **Pyramid Glasshouse**. At any time of day this is a great spot for a picnic or for smooching, although it does close respectably at dusk.

You'll recognise the **Sydney Opera House** – it sits upon **Bennelong Point** like a great crystal. Or like a basket of washing on a windy day. Or a typewriter full of oyster shells. Housing theatres, restaurants, a cinema and more, its roof shells soar to 67 metres (220 feet) and are covered by 1,000,000 tiles. See Sydney Opera House on page 40. Wander around at will, but do make sure you see the inside half of this wonder.

Landing Place of First Fleet Settlers: A covered walkway runs from the Opera House around **Sydney Cove** to **Circular Quay** (which is actually square), landing place in 1788 of the "First Fleet" settlers. "The Quay" is the hub of Sydney's ferries, and a cosmopolitan pitch of buskers, tourists and commuters. The only surviving historic building is the 1885 **Customs House**. Numerous places to snack, drink or lunch can detain you here. Watch out for a few avaricious cafes at the entrance to the ferry wharves, which charge unconscionably high sums for very ordinary food. You can spot them by the absence of any displayed prices, and by the demand for a further surcharge to "dine in", ie sit on their stools. Continue strolling in the general direction of the Harbour Bridge, around the waterfront, past the **Museum of**

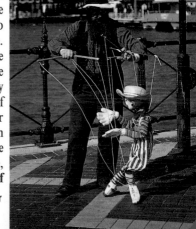

Circular Quay puppeteer

William Bligh and Cadman's Cottage

Contemporary Art and the **Overseas Passenger Terminal** and into The Rocks.

This most historic (and touristic) precinct of Sydney, **The Rocks** provides plenty to expend both money and time upon. This area (named simply after the rocky peninsula on which it was built) was the birthplace of European settlement in Australia, but its haphazard collection of hovels, brothels, wharves and bond stores has now been scrubbed up into boutiques, craft galleries and restaurants. It is most enjoyably explored by throwing away the map somewhere around the **Argyle Centre** (entrance at 18 Argyle Street) and getting lost in alleys like Suez Canal (formerly "Sewer's Canal") and Nurses Walk.

There are a number of sights in The Rocks. One, the 1816 **Cadman's Cottage** (110 George Street – just inland of the Overseas Passenger Terminal, and north of a bronze, mutiny-proof statue of Governor William Bligh) is the oldest extant residence in Australia. Despite renovations, it looks it. Further along George Street, at No 104, **The Rocks Visitors' Centre** (tel: 2474972) will provide you with current information and maps. Up Argyle Street, through the sandstone chasm of the **"Argyle Cut"**, the **Lord Nelson Hotel** (corner of Kent Street), the oldest hotel in Sydney, will provide the beer, while the **Garrison Church** (1844) deals with spirits of the other kind. The **Hero of Waterloo** (81 Windmill Street) is another historic watering hole, and on a Sunday afternoon has the world's oldest pub band, a bunch of tuneful octogenarians. (Think of them as U82.) A pub "counter lunch" (around A$10) at any pub is an unpretentious feed and a chance to meet the natives.

The bridge from the Rocks

Sydney Cove restaurants: dining with history

Audio-Visual History: Back in George Street, **The Story of Sydney** (at No 100) is an excellent one-hour audio-visual experience of Sydney from Eora Aboriginal time up to the 20th century (A$10 adults, tel: 2477777). A walk around the western shore of Sydney Cove past the **Park Hyatt Hotel**, the brilliant **Earth Exchange** mining museum (18 Hickson Road, tel: 2512422, See Museums and Art Galleries on page 43) and **Dawes Point** (where the sky is blocked by the imposing bulk of the Harbour Bridge) brings you to **Pier One**, with more fast (and slow) foods and grand harbour views, and to the much-awarded **Wharf Theatre and Restaurant** (see Dining on page 84) at Pier Four.

The bubonic plague disappeared from The Rocks 90 years ago, but no one is safe from the contagion of opals, boomerangs, designer junk and other items of antipodean excess baggage. The **Crafts Council** and **Coo-ee** gallery shops (both at 88 George Street, corner of Hickson Road) both have excellent craft wares and gifts, while the **Argyle Centre** and the **Clocktower Centre** are warrens of trinket galleries, opal shops and Australiana clothing stores. The Metcalfe Bond Storehouse (80 George Street) feature larger items such as rugs and furniture. Most of George Street from the Quay to the Bridge is a progressive boutique feast of opal jewellery, coffee, food, T-shirts and lambswool everything.

Before you spend all day and all your dollars, grab a cab for the short ride south to the **Queen Victoria Building ("QVB")**, occupying a whole block of George Street to the harbour side of the **Town Hall**. Refurbished in 1986, this is the Cinderella of Sydney architecture: an exquisite 19th-century grand design and in stone and stained glass. Almost 200 quality shops (fashion, footwear, jewellery,

leather, duty-free goods, antiques, books and crafts) line the mezzanine galleries. It's a great wander, has a silly clock on the ceiling and a stupendous Chinese jade carriage on the top floor, and on the lowest level an "Eat Street" for reasonably priced fast food with limited seating. As you tunnel your way out of the QVB's lower depths its Victorian grandeur gives way to Town Hall railway station and other street exits. It's always a surprise to see where you'll pop up.

In the next block north (ie back towards the harbour) is the 1892 **Strand Arcade** (412 George Street). With its tiered mezzanines and ironwork, this is another venerable, still beautiful, architectural dame. It connects George and Pitt Streets (between King and Market Streets). Quality jewellers, watchmakers and fashion designers trade cheek-by-jowl with coffee houses and gift shops, but for many visitors the real attraction is the building itself. A visit here is not just a re-run of the QVB – it's a reminder of Australia's early links with London.

Walk through the Strand Arcade and emerge into Pitt Street Mall. Here, the modern **Skygarden** is another superb money trap in

the guise of an architectural delight. There is a wide range of men's and women's fashion shops within this six-storey masonry mannequin, opened in 1990. (See also Shopping on page 80.) It is crowned by a fine food court (though it's rather hard to find a seat at lunchtime), restaurant and bar area known as **Skydining.**

A visit to the Observation Deck of nearby **Sydney Tower** (tel: 2333722) is the best way to take in the whole panoramic vista of Sydney, from a vantage point 305 metres (1000 feet) high. Entry is from the podium level of **Centrepoint** shopping centre (corner of Market, Pitt and Castlereagh Streets), and the lift to the top costs A$6 for adults, A$2 for children, A$14 for the family. The view is eye-boggling, especially through the

Sydney Tower, a.k.a. The Big Kebab

powerful binoculars (look down into Government House!), you may linger as long as you wish and there is plenty of information on what you are looking at. The **Sky Lounge** on the level below offers refreshments, while two revolving restaurants – one *à la carte*, one self-service – have meals that are, well, exceeded by the view.

Oxford Street links the Central Business District to the eastern suburbs. From wherever you are, catch a taxi to it while thinking about dinner. From **Whitlam Square** (corner of Liverpool, Oxford, College and Wentworth Streets) to **Taylor Square** (corner of Oxford, Bourke and Flinders Streets) and beyond, up to Paddington, Oxford Street has plenty of economical geo-culinary excursions – **Bali Inn** (No 80), **Raquel's Spanish Tavern** (98), **Tumnak Thai** (101), **The Balkan** (209) and **Borobudur** (263), plus a score more. Pricier, but well reputed, is **Streetons** (16). For thirsts and scenes there are fashion bars like the **Burdekin Hotel** (at Whitlam Square) and gay pubs **The Exchange** (34) and, just past Taylor Square, the **Albury** (6). Opposite the Albury is the **Academy Twin Cinema**, specialising in quality flicks.

Further up Oxford Street is **Paddington**. More eateries abound, from the tweely-tagged **Sloane Rangers Cafe** (No 312), to the **Landmark Cafe** (242), to the recommended fare of the **Paddington Inn** bistro (388) or the exclusive **Oasis Seros** (495), thought by many to serve Australia's most innovative cuisine.

Observation deck, Sydney Tower

Kings Cross ("The Cross") is not to everyone's taste. **Darlinghurst Road** (between William and Macleay Streets) is a flesh wound of sex clubs, junk food, hookers and lookers, and "there-but-for-the-grace-of-god-etc-etc" losers. Do *not* point your camera at most of the aforementioned, lest both camera and you be trashed. **Pink Pussycat** (38A), the **Love Machine** (60) and, across the street, **Porky's** are for ad libidinal floorshows. Pavement hucksters will give you full details of price and promised spectacle. A gamut of unmistakable sex shops offer the usual magazines and all that peculiar plumbing that is sold as "marital aids" to mostly unmarried men.

Barons Pub (upstairs, 5 Roslyn Street), with its old sofas, backgammon boards and winter fire is a welcome retreat from all this psychic tackiness, as is the **Round Midnight** jazz club opposite. A full frontal dance assault can be had at the **OzRock Pub** (corner of

Priorities

This book has been written with the intention of providing you with the authors' selection of what is the best of Sydney. However, it is unlikely that you will be able to do and see everything recommended. For those on a more restricted schedule, here is a short listing of the special highlights that every visitor to Sydney should experience. They are presented in no particular order.

- A ferry trip (preferably to Manly) or a harbour cruise.
- A visit to an Aboriginal art gallery.
- Dinner at one of the restaurants setting the pace for Australian cuisine (listed in the first half of the "Dining" chapter).
- A crossing of the Sydney Harbour Bridge – preferably on foot.
- Drinks at Watsons Bay as the sun sets down the harbour.
- Meeting a koala (at the zoo or a commercial wildlife park – see "Sydney for Kids").
- A bottle of good Australian red wine (ideally Grange Hermitage).
- A visit to a surf beach.
- A visit/tour/concert at the Opera House.

William Street and Darlinghurst Road) or the **Kardomah** (22 Bayswater Road) or **Studebakers** (19 Bayswater Road), or, if you're feeling a bit older, at the **Bourbon 'n' Beefsteak** (24 Darlinghurst Road) or its various neighbours. The **Soho Bar** (171 Victoria Street) is a trendy place to drink, while the next-door club, **The Site**, poses as hyper hip. (Reminding the great uncool that there's many a slip twixt yup and hip.)

The **Nikko Hotel** in Macleay Street has a variety of dining, drinking and shopping opportunities. In Bayswater Road, **Bayswater Brasserie** (No 32) and the **Eastside Bar and Grill** (40) provide elegant suppers. Bayswater's offshoot, Kellett Street, has a row of casual eateries of good repute (**Deans**, **Cafe Roma**, **Cafe Jax**, **ZanziBar**, **Watermelon**) co-existing in fine old terrace houses with neighbouring institutions of more dubious repute. Finish this "chock-a-block" day and night with quality coffee at **Cafe Hernandez** (60 Kings Cross Road) or, along the Darlinghurst side of Victoria Street (away from the Cross), at **Andiamo**, **Morgans** or **Nicolinas** – or try to catch someone's fancy at the **Cauldron** club (207 Darlinghurst Street).

Parks, Walks and Waves

Itineraries made for walking – through green leafy parks, bits of history, pit stops for coffee and cake, along heroic coasts, and, finally, to a good feed by the sea. (And, today, no obligatory shopping for that opal-inlaid boomerang or duty-free lambskin designer T-shirt.)

Kick off this one with a brief constitutional stroll through **Hyde Park**. Not as magnificent as its London namesake, nevertheless the leafy central aisle, which runs from the corner of Macquarie Street and St James Road, past the classical bronze figures of the **Archibald Fountain**, across Park Street, past Captain Cook (for whom the pigeons show scant respect) and on to the **ANZAC War Memorial**, is an enjoyable 10-minute stroll. The 1934 art deco War Memorial (to Australians who served in the Boer War, World War 1, World War 2, and the Korea, Malaya and Vietnam campaigns) features a dramatic sculpture of a dying soldier, also a photographic exhibition (tel: 2677668). From adjacent Liverpool or Elizabeth Streets you can catch a cab on to Centennial Park.

Centennial Park (the lungs of eastern Sydney) is most conveniently visited by car, but arrival by taxi and transferring to foot or rented bicycle is also fun. The park starts at the top end of Oxford Street,

Botanical Gardens, green and free

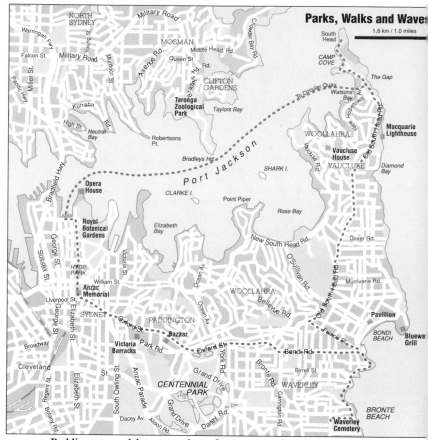

1,6 km / 1.0 miles

Paddington, and has a number of entrances. The one in York Road, Bondi Junction, provides the closest entrance to the city. Over 200 rolling hectares of lawns, trees, bridle paths, duck ponds and tranquility await you. Created in 1888 to mark Australia's first centenary, among other things the park contains a restaurant (breakfast, lunch, morning and afternoon teas), a 1988 Bicentenary pavilion and horse and bike hire facilities. Good for morning or afternoon runs or walks. Closes quaintly at sunset.

Paddington or Bondi Beach? At this point – approaching snack time – you have a choice: backtrack to Paddington (where you can also shop) or press on to Bondi Beach (where you generally don't). **Paddington**, if you're there on a Saturday, features a very good (if very 1960s) **Bazaar** in the grounds of the Uniting Church in Oxford Street: craftware, clothing, jewellery, massages, gifts and snacks – a complete "New Age meets Jimi Hendrix" experience, in fact – all at bargain prices. The rest of the street is a smorgasbord of boutiques, eateries and pubs. Try the **New Editions Bookshop** and **Tea Rooms** (328 Oxford

Paddington bookshop

Street) or the **Paddington Inn** (388). If you can spare the time, explore a few narrow side streets and their Victorian terrace houses. And if you're here on a Tuesday, drop into the Army's **Victoria Barracks** (the imposing sandstone wall in Oxford Street surrounds it) for the not to be missed, Changing-of-the-Guard ceremony at 10 am.

Bondi Beach is about 10 minutes drive further along Oxford Street and then Bondi Road. Bring your swimsuit and jump in – the water's fine between September and May, and almost bearable for a quick winter plunge. (In summer, keep an eye on your clothes when you go swimming – theft is not unknown.) The much publicised pollution of recent years has been almost eliminated. This is Australia's most famous beach, a crescent kilometre of surf, sand and exertions. The north end has a safe rock pool. In the middle is an ornate old pavilion. The south end pool features the "Icebergs" (ancient human walruses who swim year round), a radical skateboard ramp and an array of near-naked sunbathers.

Bondi also has a huge range of eating establishments, of which the **Bluewater Grill** (168 Ramsgate Avenue) on the northern point has the most spectacular site. In **Campbell Parade**, fronting the beach, try the **Lamrock Cafe** (No 72), the **Gelato Bar** (140), the new **Ramada Grand Hotel** or the superbly sited first-floor cafe at **Ravesi's Corner** (corner of Hall Street) for coffee or lunch. Fuelled up, you can now stroll the easy, shore-hugging trail which heads south for a kilometre or so, from the Icebergs Pool, around a surreal coastline of rocky coves and creamy surf to the "glamarama" of **Tamarama Beach**. Keep going to the next beach, **Bronte**, and, if you still have the legs for it, up to Waverley's picturesque old cliff-top cemetery. Here the dead all have a spectacular tomb with a view.

Hop a taxi through the well-endowed Eastern Suburbs to the harbour's southern headland, **South Head**, near **Watson's Bay**. There's a good pub (for sinking a beer or two to the sinking sun) and also several

Waverley Cemetery – tombs with a view

seafood restaurants, the most famous being **Doyle's**. But first, walk south (away from the harbour entrance) along the ocean cliff, passing a spectacular drop called **The Gap** (once Sydney's favourite suicide spot), then on to the **Macquarie Lighthouse,** which has been continually manned from 1790. Drive back along Old South Head Road, down to the harbour, then out towards the tip of this peninsula to **Camp Cove**. Most of South Head is a naval base, but further around the shore (access by foot only) from Camp Cove, you can soak up rays and/or attention at the nude beach, **Lady Jane Beach** – a scene best described as "voyeurs watching exhibitionists". The elegant 1803 **Vaucluse House** (Wentworth Road, tel: 3371957) was the home of W C Wentworth, colonial statesman and explorer. Devonshire tea is served. Open Wednesday to Sunday, 10 am to 4.30 pm. Adults, A\$4.

On weekends and public holidays, there is a ferry from Watson's Bay to Circular Quay. The last ones depart **Watson's Bay Wharf** at 6.40 pm and 6.52 pm. If you are not here in a car, extract yourself from the pub, the historic ambles, the overpriced fish 'n' chip menus and hop on board. In 40 minutes you're back in the city, having scanned the most expensive domestic real estate in the hemisphere. Rose Bay and Double Bay ("Double Pay") roll away, a close-up of the Opera House – and you're again in **Sydney Cove**. For elegant dining, try the **Rockpool** (109 George Street North) or **Bilson's** (upper level, International Terminal), the **Imperial Peking Harbourside** (115 Circular Quay West) or **Merrony's** (Quay Apartments, 2 Albert Street), none of which will let you down – unless you haven't booked.

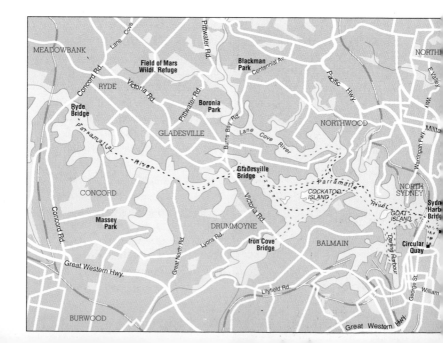

Day 3

Harbour Circuit

Today begins and ends at Circular Quay. Its adventures provide a good cross-section of everything that visitors and locals alike enjoy about Sydney: the zoo, Manly, Fort Denison, shopping and just cruising around on the water.

Many visitors to Sydney soon decide that Australians must be geometrically dyslexic: the tower of Australia Square is round while Circular Quay is rectangular. It may be argued that the actual *site* of Oz Square is quadrilateral, but we can plead historical mischance that Circular Quay has corners. It was named "Semi-

MANLY

Sydney
Harbour
Nat'l Park

Sydney
Harbour
Nat'l Park

Middle

Harbour

Spit Rd.

Grotto Pt.

Fairfax
Lookout ■

North
Head

Military Rd.

Bradleys Head Rd.

Middle
Head

MOSMAN

Sydney
Harbour
Nat'l Park

South
Head

Pacific

Taronga
Zoo ■

WATSONS
BAY

The
Gap

Ocean

CREMORNE
POINT

Sydney
Harbour
Nat'l Park

Jackson

Old South Head Rd.

Vaucluse
House ■

Macquarie
Lighthouse ■

VAUCLUSE

Port

CLARKE
ISLAND

1 Manly Ferry
2 Meadowbank Ferries
3 Five Islands Cruise
4 Harbour Lights Cruise
5 Watsons Bay Ferries
6 Main Harbour Cruise

DOUBLE
BAY

New South Head Rd.

South Head Rd.

Military Rd.

Harbour Circuit

2,4 km / 1.5 miles

Sunday juggler, at Manly Corso

circular Quay" in 1844 after landfill had been added to form a semicircular shape. Subsequent filling squared it off. Now known simply as "the Quay", it is the main departure point for the network of ferry routes around Sydney Harbour. Information on State Transit ferries can be obtained from the information booth at Circular Quay on 2474738.

A prime tour that takes you right along the main harbour is a

Harbour ferry

ferry trip to **Manly**. There are two types of ferries to Manly. The traditional one takes 33 minutes one way and costs A$3.20 (adults) and A$1.60 (children, aged four to 15) and pensioners. The newest arrivals, the Jet Cats, take a mere 12 minutes and cost A$4.30 one way with no concessions.

Allow some time to explore Manly. December 1990 marked the rebirth of **Manly Wharf** after some A$80 million was spent restoring it to the grandeur of the 1940s, when it first opened. The adjoining harbour beach has also been restored, a few of its once numerous Norfolk Island pines nurtured back to health and some 90 shops and amusement park rides shoe-horned onto the wharf. Like much of Manly, the area has a pleasant fun-in-the-sun tackiness. A nearby attraction is **Manly Oceanarium** (tel: 9492644) on West Esplanade where you travel through a giant aquarium along a moving footway within an underwater acrylic tunnel.

While in Manly, walk down the **Corso** pedestrian plaza to the long expanse of ocean beach with its surfboard riders and lifesavers. This is a good place to have lunch – the choice of restaurants is endless. However, quality and prices are not closely related. For seafood, **K's Snapper Inn** (35 South Steyne, tel: 9773880) is reasonable for both quality of its seafood and its prices. **Faulty Bowers** (7-9 Marine Parade, tel: 9775451) at Fairy Bower is another fair restaurant on a fine day. An even more picturesque location is held by **Le Kiosk** (tel: 9774122) at the edge of the sand at tiny Shelley Beach: the food is quite good, the service doesn't match the price, but the setting is superb.

The network of inner city ferries (all departing Circular Quay) stretches from Taronga Zoo to Darling Harbour and

beyond to Birkenhead Point. Fares are A$2.40 for adults and A$1.20 for children. A surprisingly pretty trip is the ferry ride up to Meadowbank, far up the Parramatta River.

Koala

Taronga Zoo (tel: 9692777, open every day from 9 am to 5 pm; access by ferry from No 2 wharf, Circular Quay) definitely has one of the best settings of any zoo in the world. Perched on a slope overlooking the harbour, it is scenically magnificent. However, there was a time when the zoo itself was an ugly place of concrete enclosures and poor conditions. This has all changed in recent years,

and it is now a model for zoological gardens everywhere. It has wildlife from around the world but is the showcase for Australian fauna. Kangaroos, wallabies, koalas and the bizarre platypus and echidna are all on display, as well as a wide range of birds, fish and reptiles.

There are regular tours out to **Fort Denison** (historically known as Pinchgut) perched on a rocky outcrop in the harbour near the Opera House. This tiny comic opera fort was originally part of Sydney's defence against a feared Russian invasion during the Crimean War (1855-1857). The rocky islet was levelled by convict labour in the 1830s and the rubble used as land fill at Circular Quay. The fort and its tower are well worth visiting and the views of the Sydney skyline are spectacular. Tours are conducted from Jetty No 6, Circular Quay, by Hegarty's Ferries at 10 am, 12.15 pm and 2 pm from Tuesday to Sunday. The cost is A$7 for adults and A$4.50 for children and pensioners. Every tour is fully escorted by a guide from the Maritime Services Board. Only 55 people can go on each tour so it is advisable to book in advance: call Hegarty's Ferries on 2472733.

A very useful way of covering the main points of Sydney Harbour is with the **Sydney Harbour Explorer** (No 6 jetty, Circular Quay, tel: 2515007) that operates every day. A day ticket costs A$15 for adults and A$9 for children and pensioners. The vessel departs Circular Quay every two hours between 9.30 am and 3.30 pm, calling at The Rocks, the Opera House, Watsons Bay, the Zoo and Darling Harbour. You can disembark and reboard when and where you like throughout the day.

Captain Cook Cruises runs some 16 harbour cruises each day. Probably the most popular is the Coffee Cruise that departs at 10 am and 2.15 pm. It's a two-and-a-half hour voyage (with commentary) along the main harbour and past the waterfront mansions of Middle Harbour in the company's most modern vessel. It costs A$20 for adults and A$12 for children and pensioners. As the name suggests, coffee and tea are served. Captain Cook Cruises can be contacted on 2515007.

Right, Circular Quay snacks

PICK & MIX

A.M. Itineraries

1. Architecture

This tour describes a horseshoe-shaped excursion from the Town Hall to Circular Quay and back to Hyde Park. Along the way much of Sydney's colonial heritage can be seen. The trip takes about an hour if you just look at the facades. However, if you plan to venture inside the places mentioned (and many are worth a closer look), you should allow a half day or more.

The start of this tour is at Queens Square, near an exit from St James railway station. It is a fitting place to begin because here you'll find three marvellous colonial Georgian buildings designed by convict architect Francis Greenway. These are **Hyde Park Barracks** (now a museum dealing with the social history of New South Wales), the **New South Wales Supreme Court** and **St James' Church**. For a good cheap lunch and an excellent overview of these, the city and the harbour visit the 14th-level cafeteria of the Law Courts opposite. It's okay, this is open to the public.

The **Mint Museum**, with its Georgian facade, is the painstakingly

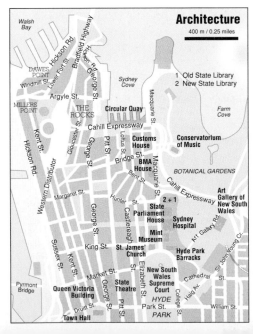

restored south wing of the old Rum Hospital, built in the 1840s and now serving as the home of numismatic and philatelic displays. It was called the Rum Hospital because the first hospital built in 1816 was paid for by granting the building contractors a lucrative monopoly on importing rum into the colony.

The enormous sandstone complex next door is **Sydney Hospital**, built in 1894 with some input from Florence Nigh-

tingale. Walk around the side of the building into the rear courtyard and check the beautiful gingerbread brick **Nightingale Building** and the antique fountain. The **State Parliament House** (open for inspection 9 am to 4.30 pm Monday to Friday, tel: 2302111) was constructed between 1810 and 1816 as part of the Rum Hospital. It has been in continual use since 1827 as the seat of government in New South Wales. Although the building may look elegant, the style of debate within is not: locally it is known as "the bearpit". An earlier state premier coined the phrase "applying a blowtorch to the belly" when discussing his welcome to a new leader of the opposition.

The **Art Gallery of New South Wales** (tel: 2251700) is a short walk across the park behind Parliament House known as the Domain. Its imposing Victorian facade and serried statues in alcoves were added to the original 1885 structure at the time of federation. The gallery is open from 10 am to 5 pm except on Sunday when the hours are 12 noon to 5 pm. It houses a strong collection of Australian works and a weaker number of dark and foreboding European paintings. There are always special exhibitions on display – check the Saturday *Sydney Morning Herald* for details. The Art Gallery Restaurant (tel: 2325425, open for lunch only) is very good and relatively inexpensive but the service can be patchy.

Towards the southern end of Macquarie Street is the new **State Library**, opened in 1988. It's a pleasant place to visit and is open from 9 am to 9 pm from Monday to Saturday and 2 pm to 6 pm on Sunday. It is joined by an enclosed overhead pedestrian bridge to the old **State Library** (tel: 2301414), often known as the Mitchell Library, housed in one of the most impressive buildings in Sydney. The main reading room is an airy hall, naturally lit by an imposing skylight.

Across the road at 135-137 Macquarie Street stands a pinnacle of Sydney's art deco buildings: the **BMA** (British Medical Association) **House**,

The Conservatorium of Music

built in 1930. The elaborate facade of this building is truly wonderful and well worth a look. Note the fine details like its stone koalas.

Walking down Macquarie Street towards the Opera House and the harbour, the park on your right is the **Botanical Gardens.** This well tended swathe of greenery with its duck ponds and hidden groves can provide a pleasant break from the concrete and traffic of the city. The castellated structure in Macquarie Street, right at the city entrance to the Cahill Expressway, is the **Conservatorium of Music** (tel: 2301222). This unusual building is open to the public – concerts take place here regularly. The "Con" building looks far too elaborate for its present purpose – it is even more incongruous to think that it was originally built as the stables for nearby Government House.

Turning left from Macquarie Street into Albert Street, you walk down a short steep hill to Circular Quay. Sadly, the only surviving historic building along the Quay is the **Customs House**, between Young and Loftus Streets. It is reputedly located where the Union Jack was flown for the first time in Sydney Cove. For passersby, the most notable feature of this 1885 building is the intricately carved stone coat-of-arms over the entrance and the decidedly unamused visage of Queen Victoria above the door.

Across Alfred Street and under the remarkably ugly Cahill Expressway and Circular Quay railway station stands **Circular Quay**. The Cahill Expressway seemed like a great step forward in transport when it was built in 1958 and named after a New South Wales premier. Now it is rightly seen as an eyesore that cuts the city off from the harbour. To the western (or Harbour Bridge) side of the Quay is the classic but monolithic Art Deco building which once housed the Maritime Services Board. It is now the Museum of Contemporary Art.

Upon reaching George Street, skip **The Rocks** (the area up to your right) at this time and walk up George Street a few blocks past Wynyard Station to Market

Street. The **State Theatre** (49 Market Street, tel: 2642431) between George and Pitt Streets is an astonishingly ornate picture palace built in 1929. Although it is obviously better if the movie playing is one you want to see, the statues, chandeliers and marble staircase inside this flamboyant gilded structure ensure that any visit will leave an indelible impression.

Returning to George Street, cross the road and enter the vast **Queen Victoria Building** (QVB) that occupies a complete city block. For years the QVB was a ugly blot on the cityscape: a few shops clung to a tenuous existence at street level and the dingy interior housed the Sydney City Library. Then it closed for a few years then in 1986 it emerged, chrysalis-like, from the renovator's scaffolding, irradiated by the A$75 million allegedly spent on it. Both the shops and structure of the QVB compete for your attention. The basement level has the inevitable array of food outlets in an "Eats Street".

A good finishing point for this tour is the **Town Hall**, on the corner of George and Park streets, with its startling mixture of styles

reflecting the several architects who worked on it before it opened in 1889 and on extensions thereafter. Irrespective of aesthetics, it is an imposing building and the Town Hall steps are a favourite meeting place for Sydneysiders. Inside is a fascinating blend of marble and crystal chandeliers; plus the very impressive, but sadly under-utilised, six-keyboard, 8,500-pipe grand organ (recently restored) – and truly terrible acoustics, a fact long rued by Town Hall concert-goers.

2. Sydney Opera House

Whether you go to see a show, have dinner, take a tour or merely walk around it, every visitor to Sydney should look over the Opera House. Despite the somewhat unfinished look inside the shell, it is a remarkable structure in a spectacular setting.

It is important to bear in mind that the Sydney Opera House is a public building. In a way, its world-famous profile is only a secondary aspect – this is no mere monument to be viewed from afar. Rather, you are welcome to attend performances at any of its

Architectural Amblings

Visitors with time to venture further afield should include Elizabeth Bay House and, at Parramatta, the governor's country residence, and Elizabeth Farm House in their itineraries. **Elizabeth Bay House** (7 Onslow Avenue, Elizabeth Bay, tel: 3582344, open Tuesday to Sunday 10 am to 4.30 pm) is a superb 1835 Regency mansion with a stunning interior and great views of the harbour.

Parramatta, the second settlement established in the colony, contains many historic buildings. **Old Government House** (tel: 6358149), which was built in 1790 and extended by governors Hunter and Macquarie in the following 26 years, is now a museum containing 19th-century Australian furniture. Located in Parramatta Park, the house was the official vice-regal country residence of the period and is the country's oldest public building. **Elizabeth Farm House** (70 Alice Street, tel: 6359488, open Tuesday to Sunday 10 am to 4.30 pm), begun in 1793 and containing parts of Australia's oldest surviving European building, was the residence of merino sheep farmers, John and Elizabeth Macarthur. Macarthur dominated colonial society and his house was an important social centre for the colony. Today it is a museum furnished in early colonial style.

theatres: the Opera Theatre (that can seat 1,500), the Concert Hall (2,700), the Drama Theatre (550) and various other halls accommodating between 150 and 420 people. Or you can dine in one of several restaurants, drink at one of the bars, or merely walk around the building and inside it and admire the vision of its designer. You won't be alone – about half of all visitors to Australia visit the sail-like structure on Bennelong Point.

The Opera House looks so right in its setting that it is hard to remember that it replaced a dilapidated set of tram sheds incongruously located on a prime piece of real estate at the eastern end of Circular Quay. Its creator conceived the striking design after only seeing photographs of the site.

In 1957, the New South Wales government conducted a world-wide competition for the design of an opera house. Some 220 entries were received but one by a 38-year-old Danish architect named Jørn Utzon stood out. Art critic Robert Hughes has described that original design as little more than "a magnificent doodle" but the white sails soaring above the harbour were a vision which showed genius in more than spectacle alone. Columnless performance spaces, stage mechanisms located vertically above and below the proscenium and the promise of impeccable perfect acoustics were all innovations that convinced the international judging panel.

Utzon and his team began to translate the schematic vision into concrete and steel in 1959 with a projected completion date of 1963. However, construction was slow, the political backbiting was intense, and the price rose more quickly than its 67-metre (220-foot) high sails. Even though the building was paid for by state-run lotteries, Utzon was ordered to reduce the ever-growing budget by working with a team of government architects. He refused to compromise and in 1966 quit the project and Australia. "Tear it down" was his parting shot – he has never seen the completed building.

He would have had to wait a while to do so. The flawed masterpiece was opened on 20 October 1973 by Queen Elizabeth in one of those grand harbourside occasions that Sydney does so well. The major performance on that opening night was of

Opera House

Beethoven's Ninth Symphony. The final reckoning revealed that the building had cost A$102 million and taken 19 years to complete: a far cry from the original estimates of A$7 million and five years.

Today, with all the acrimony in the past, Sydney is justifiably proud of the Opera House. Its statistics remain awesome. The roof sections weigh 158,000 tons and are supported by 350 kilometres (217 miles) of cables. Over 6,200 square metres (67,000 square feet) of tinted French glass enclose its "Space Gothic" interiors. The Concert Hall organ, with 10,500 pipes, is the largest mechanical-action organ in the world. The whole complex covers 1.8 hectares (4.5 acres). The one million anti-fungal roof tiles never need cleaning. And, as Utzon intended, the acoustics in the Opera Theatre are regarded as "perfect" (although the orchestra pit is too small for many purposes).

To select a performance to attend at the Opera House, consult the entertainment sections of the daily newspapers or call the Opera House box office on 2507777. The Opera House is not the exclusive domain of those who can afford the top-priced opera tickets. Within its spectacular shell is a varied offering of drama, cinema, dance, orchestral recitals, rock concerts, conferences, exhibitions, outdoor concerts and more. There is considerable variety every day attracting over 1.6 million spectators each year.

A great event for the visitor is "An Evening at the Sydney Opera House", which includes a guided tour, dinner and a performance of opera, dance, ballet, music or theatre. Prices range from A$70 to A$100, depending upon the performance. Book through the Opera House's Tourism Marketing section or, if flying Qantas, through its overseas offices.

Forecourt restaurant, Opera House

Organized tours run each day between 9 a.m and 4 p.m. and cost A$6 for adults. On Sundays there are backstage tours for the same price. Bookings can be made by calling 2507250.

There are three restaurants at the Opera House. The most informal is the **Forecourt** (tel: 2507300) that serves upmarket sandwiches, light meals and great desserts along with a selection of wines and cocktails. At the very tip of Bennelong Point, the **Harbour Restaurant** (tel: 2507191) like the Forecourt is best experienced sitting outside on a summer afternoon. It is the complex's mid-priced restaurant offering reasonable value for money and scenic splendour. High dining at the Opera House is in the **Bennelong** restaurant (tel: 2507578) within its own sail-capped building on the "wrong" side of the complex, away from the harbour. It is open for lunch and dinner every day except Sunday. Meals are quite expensive but the standard of service and food is very good. In this sublime setting, with a pianist to entertain you on Thursday, Friday or Saturday nights, it can be a special experience. It is not every day that you dine inside a national symbol.

3. Museums and Art Galleries

Lay Sydney's museums and art galleries end-to-end and they would stretch further than a visitor's attention span. The following are but a few of the closest and the most interesting from which to chose for one morning of saturation acculturation.

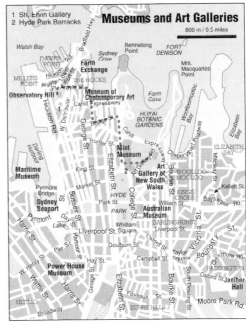

Observatory Hill, in The Rocks area, is an appropriate starting point to a Sydney culture cruise. The city's highest natural point, with a spectacular view of Port Jackson, it was the site first of a windmill (1796), then a half-built fort (1803) and finally, in 1848, a shipping signal station. The signal station survives as the **Sydney Observatory**, but its era for studying the little-known southern sky has passed, city pollution now making serious astronomical study impossible. Today it is the **Museum of Astronomy** (tel: 2412478), open Monday to Friday, 2 pm to 5 pm, Saturday and Sunday, 10 am to 5 pm. Most evenings it conducts night-sky observation sessions for lay skywatchers (bookings are necessary and entry is A$5 for adult, A$2 for kids).

On the same hill above The Rocks, Governor Macquarie built a military hospital in 1815. It is now the **National Trust Centre** and includes the **S H Ervin Gallery** (Watson Road, tel: 2580174), one of the largest non-commercial galleries in Sydney, specialising in the very best Australian figurative art.

Also in The Rocks, the revolutionary **Earth Exchange** geological and mining museum (18 Hickson Road, tel: 2512422) is an interactive, audio-visual trip through the Earth's mineral and fossil history, with an emphasis on Australian minerals, plus a simulated underground mine. Open every day, 10 am to 5 pm (adults A$6.50, children A$5), the Earth Exchange features Australia's best mineral collection, a simulation of a Sydney earthquake and Australia's largest extant gold nugget. The gift shop stocks a wide variety of gemstones (including opals), minerals and related books.

Holdsworth Gallery, Paddington

For art that is always up to the moment but never out of date, see the very new **Museum of Contemporary Art** (132 George Street, tel: 2524033) at Circular Quay, which displays a collection of over 4,000 Australian and international contemporary art works, housed in a 1940s art deco building.

Five minutes' drive away from The Quay, up on Macquarie Street, is the **Mint Museum**, a painstakingly restored wing of the 1816 "Rum Hospital". (In those days the economy of the young colony literally floated on rum, the de facto currency. Governor William Bligh – of *Bounty* fame – experienced another rebellion when he attempted to mop up these "liquid assets".) In 1851 this building became the first branch of the Royal Mint outside London, and produced gold coins until 1927. It is now a museum of Australian decorative arts, coins and stamps. Entry costs A$5 for adult, A$5 for children and A$12 for families. (Tel: 2170333. Open daily 10 am-5 pm, except Wednesday, 12 noon-5 pm.) The neighbouring Georgian-style **Hyde Park Barracks** was commissioned by Governor Macquarie in 1819 and designed by convict architect Francis Greenway. It is now a museum of the social history of New South Wales from convict days to the 1950s, with displays on themes of immigration, public celebrations and the founding of Australia. (Tel: 2170333. Open daily 10 am-5 pm, except Tuesdays 12 noon-5 pm.)

A short walk across the Domain parkland from Macquarie Street brings you to the **Art Gallery of New South Wales** (in Art Gallery Road). Its Classical facade belies the flexibility and breadth of the

Decorated Aboriginal wood-winds

Australian, international and Asian collections within. Be sure to see the Aboriginal and Papua New Guinean tribal art. (Open Monday-Saturday, 10 am-5 p.m, Sunday, 12 noon-5 pm. Tel: 2251700.)

The **Australian Museum** (corner of William and College Streets, tel: 3398111) holds the country's largest collection of natural history (marine life, birds, mammals etc) exhibits and an excellent Aboriginal Australia display. (Admission adults A$5 and children A$2, Open Tuesday to Saturday, 10 am to 5 pm; Sunday and Monday, 12 noon to 5 pm. Tel: 3398111.) A 10-minute car ride to Paddington brings you to **Juniper Hall** (248 Oxford Street). This grand 1824 mansion, recently restored to its original glory by the National Trust, now serves as the **Australian Museum of Childhood** with displays of toys, dolls and books. It's a gentle, low-key place, but worth a look for the architecture and for a glance back to days when kids did not need a cruise missile (or even Tom Cruise) for Christmas. Open 10 am-4 pm daily.

Back across town, just west of Darling Harbour, is the superstar of Sydney museums, the **Power-house Museum** (500 Harris Street, Ultimo). This 1899 power station and former tram depot has been renovated to house the huge collection of the Museum of Applied Arts and Sciences. Dynamic displays involve the visitor in "hands-on" experience. Four major themes — science,

Australian Museum of Childhood, Paddington

technology, decorative arts and social history – encompass such apparitions as the state's first train engine, bush kitchens and art deco interiors, planes and even a space shuttle. Allow *plenty* of time for this one – kids love it and it loves them. (Tel: 2170111. Open 10 am to 5 pm daily. Admission A$5 for adults, A$2 for kids and A$12 for families.)

Darling Harbour has two nautical museums, both on the western shore. Beneath the sail-like roofs of the new **National Maritime Museum** is an exciting recreation of Australia's long maritime history. **Sydney Seaport** can be easily identified by the partially restored hull of the old grain clipper *James Craig*, a 12-metre yacht and the vintage ferry *Kanangra*. (Tel: 5522011. Open daily 10 am-5 pm. Adults A$2.)

Commercial Art Galleries: These are numerous and cater to all tastes in art, from outback kitsch to postmodern obsessive. Check the *Sydney Morning Herald* listings on Friday ("Metro" section) or Saturday for details, or see the yellow pages. Many private galleries are to be found in the Paddington-Woollahra area. For contemporary Australian painting, sculpture and installation, check **Robin Gibson**, **Julie Green**, **Macquarie**, **Mori**, **Gary Anderson** or **Ivan Dougherty** galleries. For photography, visit the **Australian Centre for Photography**, 257 Oxford Street, Paddington, tel: 3316253, 3321455. For Aboriginal art, the best traditional art is in the **Art Gallery of New South Wales** and the **Australian Museum**. Purchasable work (bark paintings, didgeridoos, coolamon carriers etc.) may be found at numerous outlets (see Shopping, on page 80).

4. The Spit to Manly Harbour Walk

An easy, eight-kilometre (five-mile) trail leads around the northern foreshores of Sydney Harbour from the Spit Bridge to Manly Wharf. In places this unparallelled eyeful of Australian bush and bay scenery is much as Captain Phillip would have seen it.

Grab a sunny day and a pair of light walking shoes, a sunhat and water bottle, and head out for three hours of coastal foot cruising. **"The Spit"** (that is, "sandspit") is located about 30 minutes north of the city, via North Sydney, Neutral Bay, Mosman and Spit Junction. Government buses from York Street in the city will get you here, but it will be far quicker to catch a taxi for about A$20. After arriving at the northern end of the **Spit Bridge**, cross the road to the eastern side, descend to a grassy clearing (from which the pre-bridge punts used to cross), then follow the path east around the foreshore. Generally well marked, the trail becomes temporarily obscure in only one or two places – if so, just retrace your footsteps and look again.

Manly Wharf

Leaf-framed views of sandstone headlands, ultramarine-gone-ultraviolet views of harbour expanse, sails and ferry wakes, bomboras (reef waves), buoys and picnic coves – all these can delight the hiker. Bring a swimming costume and take a dip from time to time, although in summer be mindful of sharks. (It has been a quarter of a century since the last fatal attack inside the harbour, but why risk becoming a footnote in history?)

As you amble (and there really is no rush), you will pass the front lawns of sumptuous houses, but as culture surrounds nature – and this seems odd – you will see almost no birds or fauna, and certainly no kangaroos or koalas. Nevertheless, nature at least will not shrink any further here, for much of the trail runs through sections of **Sydney Harbour National Park**. In parts there is evidence of bushfires: these happen infrequently, and only in high summer – although in 1990 a Japanese tour group had the thrill of being rescued from a fire in this area by a helicopter evacuation. Along the way illustrated plaques inform you about nearby native flora, such as grevillea, figs, banksia, scentless rosewood, angophora, wandering jew and "black boys", all of which are protected (so don't pick them).

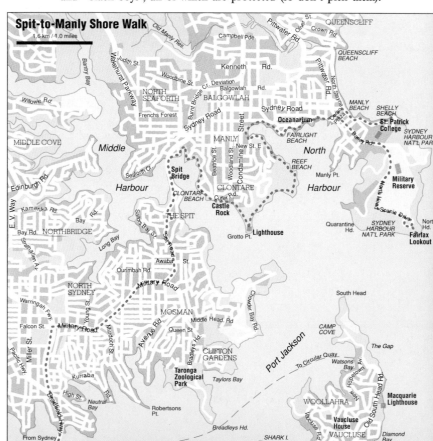

Spit-to-Manly Shore Walk

1.6 km / 1.0 miles

The first section of the walk, 1.4 kilometres (less than a mile) to **Clontarf Beach**, takes about 40 minutes, skirting a shady bay before arriving at Clontarf, which has shark-proof swimming, picnic facilities and road access. (It is possible to cover only portions of this walk, exiting where the trail meets a local road, such as at Beatty Street, Balgowlah – though here you'll be a long way from public transport or taxis.) Continue on to **Castle Rock** and **Grotto Point**, site of a pretty lighthouse that from afar looks like a tiny Greek island chapel. From close up it is far less interesting, but the point it sits upon gives a great view of what one of the "First Fleeters" described as "the finest harbour in the universe". On a clear day you can see what he meant.

This is approaching the halfway point on the trek: about 3.2 kilometres (2 miles) and 1.25 hours. There are nearby Aboriginal carvings, which you may stumble upon if you are lucky. They are not signposted in order

Middle Harbour

to avoid the graffiti of contemporary "yobbo" tribesmen. Easier to spot is **Washaway Beach** below Grotto Point, a nudist beach and a good place for a swim. Next come **Crater Cove**, **Dobroyd Point** (spot the tiny rock huts in the cove – fishermen and hippies have lived in them for years) and **Reef Beach**, the latter being another nudist beach. When you hit **Forty Baskets Beach** the modest attire of the swimmers signals the end of the "wild" part of the walk. From here on it's mainly a suburban stroll for the next half hour around the foreshores of **Fairlight**.

What Captain Phillip Thought: This potted view of the Australian bush now gives way to the leisure possibilities of Manly – named so because this is what Captain Phillip of the First Fleet thought of the local Aborigines. (In fact, they were so bloody manly that they speared him!) Manly has an **Oceanarium** (Tel: 9492644) on West Esplanade, where a moving footway takes you through a transparent tunnel above which fish and sharks swim, a fine **Art Gallery** (also on West Esplanade), a newly polished-up ferry wharf (plus ferris wheel, bars, restaurants, shops), a cinema, and of course great harbour and ocean beaches.

After a refreshing ale, coffee or juice at **Manly Wharf**, if there's some kick left in your heels, head east on the **Corso**. This street runs the few hundred metres from the harbour to the ocean beach, past a

Manly Corso – buskers, beers and boardshorts

surfeit of take-away food joints, pseudo-Scandinavian ice-cream shops, pubs and some real hit-and-miss restaurants. (If reheated crêpes served without apology are your idea of a hit then you won't want to miss some of these places.) Among Manly's many other eating options – not all of them may be open for lunch – are **Tamnam Thai** (opposite Manly Wharf), Japanese food at **Kamome's**, more Thai at **Somi's** and the up-market **Gilbert's** in the Manly Pacific Parkroyal Hotel.

And then you're at **South Steyne**, facing the great Pacific Ocean and the famous expanse of surf and sand which is **Manly Beach**. The once stately, now balding Norfolk Island pines attest to the ravages of atmospheric pollution, detergents and salt. On Sundays a market is held here on the esplanade, with the usual ceramic, leather and bric-a-brac offerings. Facing the sea, to your left – at the far end of the beach – is **Queenscliff**, and to your right the cove of **Shelley Beach**, the point and surf of **Fairy Bower**, and the **North Head** of Sydney Harbour. The Gothic-looking stone building on the hill is **St Patrick's College**. For more information about this lovely suburb, drop into the

Manly Cove Beach

Bushwalking, harbour shore

Manly Visitors Information Bureau, South Steyne. Tel: 9771088.

Keep walking south (that is, to your right) along the esplanade to the South Steyne Surf Club, then around the ocean-side path, where after five minutes you'll reach **Fawlty Bowers Cafe** (7 Marine Parade, tel: 9775451) and a well-earned lunch. The food is fresh and unpretentious. If you're feeling in the mood for seafood, continue walking for another few minutes to **Le Kiosk** (Marine Parade, tel: 9774122) at Shelley Beach, preferably having booked beforehand.

Return to Manly by the same route, or if you have time by taxi take a quick look at **North Head**, the gem of the Sydney Harbour National Park. **Fairfax Lookout** at the point provides a great view. Back towards Manly, on the harbour side, is the defunct 1833 **Quarantine Station**, which is now administered as a tourist attraction. (Call 9776229 for bookings.) After this very crowded morning, return to Circular Quay in the city from Manly Wharf, rapidly by Jet-Cat, or more placidly by ferry.

P.M. Itineraries

1. Harbour Bridge to North Sydney

The pedestrian walkway on the eastern side of the Harbour Bridge is perhaps Sydney's most under-utilised free tourist attraction: the walk to the North Shore is memorable and puts the massive scale of the bridge into true proportion. If you catch a train or ferry back from Milsons Point/Kirribilli, the return trip can take as little as two hours but it is better to allocate more time. The best time to take this walk is at dawn as the sun rises between Sydney Heads and turns the harbour to liquid gold.

The place to start this tour is **Dawes Point Park** directly under the bridge in The Rocks. This provides a daunting worm's-eye view of the monumental structure. Spare a thought for the architects and engineers who stood here in the 1920s and envisaged a span reaching across the deep harbour.

The bridge was built from both ends, starting in 1923 and joining in 1930. The stone pylons are largely decorative and the arch is supported by four huge pins each 35 centimetres (14 inches) in diameter and 4.16 metres (13.6 feet) long. The total weight of steel in the 300,000 bridge is 53,000 tonnes. It takes

10 years to paint the bridge and the task consumes over 30,000 litres (60,600 gallons) of paint. (Ask Paul Hogan, he used to be a rigger on the Bridge.)

To access the bridge's eastern walkway walk to Cumberland Street at the top of the Argyle steps off Argyle Street. (Bicycle riders will be glad to know that there is a cycleway on the western side of the bridge looking westwards.) Once onto the walkway, your path is clear, as is your view, although only a short way along you'll notice that a block of flats intrudes upon your view down the harbour. This is subsidised housing provided by the government – and in turn providing some of the best residential views in Sydney. This building was a point of some contention among Sydneysiders.

But then, nearly everything in Sydney is both political and controversial. It was under the shadow of political turmoil in the Great Depression that the Sydney Harbour Bridge was opened in March 1932. Just as the structure has become an enduring part of the city landscape, the opening ceremony has become an embarrassing part of Australian history. Before state Premier Jack Lang could ceremonially cut the ribbon to open the bridge, Captain de Groot of the paramilitary New Guard rode up and slashed it with his sword, declaring the bridge open on behalf of "the decent and loyal citizens of New South Wales". The ribbon was eventually retied and the official ceremony continued. However, the political frame could not be so easily reconstructed: within a couple of months, Lang had been dismissed from office by the governor and the far right of New South Wales politics had prevailed.

The south-eastern pylon of the bridge is open to the public from Saturday to Tuesday between 10 am and 5 pm in winter and every day in summer. Inside there is an historical display on the building of the bridge and, at the top of a 200-step climb, a wonderful panorama of Sydney.

North Sydney Olympic Swimming Pool

The admission fee is A$1 for adults and A$0.50 for children.

Unfortunately, the top of the arch of the bridge is not open to the public, although Sydney's newspapers regularly report on the exploits of brave souls who climb it only to be arrested upon their descent.

North Sydney is the ever-growing centre for much of Sydney's media and advertising industry. These high-profile industries are well supported by several upmarket shopping centres and stylish restaurants. **Armstrongs Brasserie** (1-7 Napier Street, North Sydney, tel: 9552066) serves the multinational polyglot hotchpotch often described as modern Australian cuisine. It's a good brasserie combining a fresh decor with imaginative cooking. Alternatively, the **Malaya** in the old fire station at 86 Walker Street (tel: 9554306) is relatively culturally pure, right down to the rather casual service. It has a pleasantly refreshing modern decor and there are some bland dishes on the menu, but if your system needs a chilli steam-clean order a *laksa*. It looks like soup but tastes like lava.

After a brisk stroll across the bridge (or an incendiary *laksa*), the perfect way to finish up is to walk down to **North Sydney Olympic Swimming Pool** almost under the northern end of the bridge. The pool has been the scene of some memorable moments in Australia's sporting history, but that's not the main reason to visit. In winter, there is a heat-retaining bubble erected over the pool and the view is restricted. However, in summer this is an excellent place to swim and sightsee concurrently – especially if you swim backstroke. Floating on the water and watching the trains cross the bridge overhead provides an unusual perspective on city transport patterns. Watching the peak hour crowds stuck in heavy bridge traffic while you wallow balmily below is the icing on the cake.

2. A Pub Crawl

To get "blotto" is not the point of this itinerary, although it may be an occupational hazard. Drink light beer or lemon squash to maintain the regimen. A tour of these watering holes gives you a glimpse, first, of ordinary Australians (with no "Crocodile Dundee Goes Duty-Free" acts), and, second, of some of the social history woven into – or formulated in – Sydney's pubs.

To begin at Sydney's beginnings ... in **The Rocks**, there are the **Lord Nelson Hotel** (corner of Kent and Argyle Streets), the oldest hotel in town, and now a bar, brasserie and brewery,

Old-style beer delivery – The Rocks

the **Fortune of War Hotel** (137 George Street) which occupies the oldest hotel *site* in Sydney (it was built in 1922, replacing its 1839 namesake), and the **Hero of Waterloo** (81 Windmill Street), also a contender for the title of oldest pub. The Hero's cellars were reputedly used as holding cells for "press-ganged" sailors back in the "roaring days". All around are the Victorian-era houses of Lower Fort Street and great wooden wharf sheds of Walsh Bay's Hickson Road.

Alcohol Culture: But wait, already! A word on Sydney alcohol culture. The colony of New South Wales was founded on rum, and by 1808 (the time of Governor William Bligh of *Bounty* fame), it was the quasi-official currency. However, beer, "the amber fluid", is now Australia's favourite tipple – Australia has even been called "the Land of the Liquid Lunch" – and it has its own vocabulary. "Tinnies" are tin cans, "twisties" are twist-top bottles, "stubbies" are also bottles. Fosters, Tooheys, Coopers, Castlemaine XXXX (pronounced "Four Ex" – reputedly because Queenslanders can't spell "beer") and Swan are some of the main brands, followed by the "boutique" beers, Hahn, Eumundi, Redback, Dogbolter etc. Also available, but more expensive, are imports like

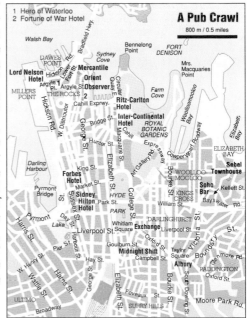

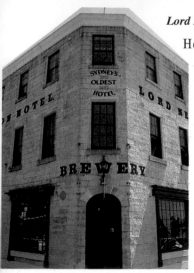

Lord Nelson Hotel

Heineken, NZ Steinlager, Corona, Guinness and so on. Australian beers are generally far higher in alcohol content than standard British or American brews, and in pubs are served very cold. The "middy", which costs around A$1.20 and up, is a manageable-sized beer of about half a pint, but drinking the larger "schooner", around A$1.60 and up, is not going to get you through today's agenda if you sink one at each stop.

For a change of "neck oil", try Queensland's Bundaberg rum, commonly referred to as "Bundy". Australia also produces excellent wines, but these are not served by the glass over the counter, although they can be purchased by the bottle. "House" wine by the glass will be the *ordinaire* but passable "Château Cardboard", that is, from a boxed cask.

While Australian pub culture is unmistakably male, all pubs have mixed drinking – although in some women may prefer not to tread. In all pubs mentioned herein, visitors – male and female – should feel quite at ease.

Meanwhile, back in George Street in The Rocks ... move into the post-convict era at either the Orient, Observer or Mercantile Hotels. The re-gentrified **Orient** (corner of Argyle Street) is a familiar after-five meeting place for office workers and professionals and serves good food. The more proletarian **Mercantile** (No 25) has a distinctly Irish flavour and often features folk singers – and Guinness-fuelled riotous times on St. Patrick's Day or Melbourne Cup Day. The **Observer** (No 25) is equally welcoming and "fair dinkum" Australian. In The Rocks' sea of ersatz Oz, the latter two places are sanctuary for the sort of ordinary Australians for whom "duty-free" means nothing more than a day off work and who wouldn't be caught dead at the "barby" in some dorky Ken Done apron.

Up in **Macquarie Street** there are two hotels (you'd never call them "pubs") which architecturally symbolise Sydney of the late 20th century – by glueing it onto 19th-century buildings. Both are five-star international chain hotels, featuring the nostalgia and elegant schizophrenia of "facade-ism". The **Ritz-Carlton** (No 93) has sprung, miraculously cured, out of the bricks of a former VD clinic and hospital, while the much larger **Inter-Continental** (No 117) sprouts from the shell of the once lovely sandstone Colonial Treasury Building. In the former establishment, sink something like a stout or port in the clubby instant antiquity of **The Bar.** In the latter, tea in the central courtyard is quite genteel, but even ordinary whisky in the lounge bar on level 34 is breath-taking. The view stretches from the

Sydney Domain, through the Harbour Heads and almost to New Zealand. The prices too are elevated, but with a vista like this it's a bargain high.

Back down to earth, the **Forbes Hotel** (corner of York and King Streets) is another piece of renovated history, but without the high-rise implant. Lots of polished wood, brass and stained glass in this colonial Central Business District boozer and eatery. Today it's pretty yuppie – not a coachman, cooper or trooper to be seen – but a good place to rub shoulders with after-workers.

Five minutes walk away in George Street (opposite the Queen Victoria Building), in the bowels of the **Sydney Hilton Hotel**, is the extraordinary **Marble Bar**. So precious a creation is this 1893 darling that it was dismantled, then reassembled marble panel by gilt gee-gaw when its original home, the George Adams Hotel, was removed in the early 1970s to make way for the Hilton. It is all green marble chintz, original paintings, stained glass, ornate columns and an indicator of the great wealth which poured through Sydney in the last century. Lots of jazz and rock played here. Opens at 4 pm.

Doorman, Ritz-Carlton

As night closes in you can check out the gay pubs in **Oxford Street**, notably **The Exchange** (No 34), **Midnight Shift** (No 85) and in Paddington the **Albury** (No 6). They're flamboyant (and "glamboyant"), and the last has raucous, camped-up entertainment. In King's Cross the **Celebrities Bar** in the **Sebel Townhouse** (23 Elizabeth Bay Road) is intimate, fairly hetero-, and you might even catch sight of the stars and entertainers who regularly patronise the hotel. The **Soho Bar** in the **Piccadilly** pub (171 Victoria Street) is younger, less formal (to get in wear black, Darlinghurst's universal non-colour) and a good example of Sydney pub deco architecture.

Finally, Harold Park Hotel (115 Wigram Road, Glebe) has "Writers in the Park" every Tuesday evening. Some of Australia's best (and least) known writers read their works in this quintessentially Oz "tiles-and-track" pub, adjacent to the Harold Park "trots" (or harness racing track).

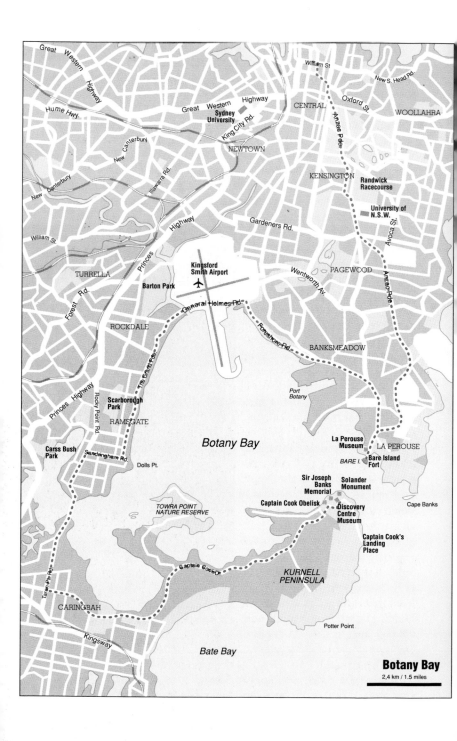

Botany Bay

2,4 km / 1.5 miles

3. Botany Bay

Here's a chance to get out of the city (though not out of Sydney), to cross the great red-tiled suburban sea and to arrive, yet again, at the ocean. Combining wilderness, historical sites and a contemporary industrial "frightscape", Botany Bay is where "white" Australia began, with Captain Cook and all that ...

You'll need a car for this one. Starting at **Taylor Square** (in Oxford Street), drive south from the city along **ANZAC Parade**. This long avenue passes a number of sacred sporting sites, the **Sydney Cricket Ground, Moore Park Golf Course, Randwick Racecourse**, and the **University of New South Wales**. Through **Maroubra**, continue south until you hit **La Perouse** on the northern arm of Botany Bay. The 16-kilometre (10-mile) drive from Sydney takes about 30 minutes.

Windswept **Botany Bay** is where European Australia hiccoughed to life, when, at 3 pm on 29 April 1770, James Cook, RN, stepped ashore from the *Endeavour* to assay the "Great South Land" for Britain. The place was named Botany Bay after more than 3,000 new botanical specimens were collected by the expedition's naturalist, Joseph Banks. Australia's most famous convict ballad, *Botany Bay*, was inspired by the fearful reputation of this place. In 1788, the First Fleet anchored here briefly, found the site unsuitable for a permanent settlement, and moved to Sydney Cove, a better-watered site on an excellent harbour that Cook had overlooked.

The **La Perouse Monument and Museum** commemorate the stay in Botany Bay in 1788 of a small French fleet commanded by explorer the Comte de La Perouse, who arrived only six days behind Captain Arthur Phillip and the First Fleet. (After sailing from Botany Bay, La Perouse's ships apparently disappeared off the face of the earth, until their wreckage was discovered in the Solomon Islands in 1828.) The **Old Cable Station** (1881) was built for the undersea telegraph line to New Zealand, and now houses the **La Perouse Museum** and an **Aboriginal Art Gallery**. (ANZAC Parade, La Perouse, tel:

ANCHORING THE 'ENDEAVOUR'

In front of you out on the bay, approximately 500 metres away, there is a red buoy. This is the site where Captain James Cook anchored the 'Endeavour' in 1770.

The Maritime Services Board now maintains this site as one of its navigational markers for ships entering Botany Bay.

Kurnell: Where it all began

La Perouse Museum

6612765. Open daily 10 am-4.30 pm.) Nearby is the 1820s **Macquarie Watchtower**, the oldest existing building on the bay, erected by Governor Macquarie to house soldiers attempting to control smuggling in Botany Bay. A nearby grave is of Père Receveur, a Franciscan monk on La Perouse's expedition.

On Sunday afternoon this is a lively area, with the local Aborigines, migrant families, picnickers, sightseers all enjoying the open spaces and fresh air. There is even a snake tamer's show (from 1.30 pm) in the little metal enclosure near the last bus stop. Linked by a bridge to the shore is **Bare Island Fort**. The fort was constructed in 1881, in anticipation of French or Russian attacks, and its barracks added in 1889. The foes did not materialise, so the guns have never been fired in anger.

On the southern arm of the bay, **Kurnell Peninsula**, now the home of huge oil refineries, is the site of **Captain Cook's Landing Place**. Located 36 kilometres (22 miles) south of Sydney, it is reached by driving from La Perouse along Foreshore Road, General Holmes Drive, the Grand Parade, Taren Point Road and Captain Cook Drive. (This will take about 20 minutes, which can be broken by a drink at the **Resort Hotel Brighton**.)

Monuments which commemorate the eight days Cook spent at Kurnell include the **Captain Cook Obelisk** (erected in 1870); the **Sir Joseph Banks Memorial** (1947); the **Solander Monument** (1914) and a tablet to the memory of **Seaman Forby Sutherland**, the first European definitely known to be buried on the continent. All of these are more historical than spectacular, but the site is perfect for a quiet picnic, with views across the broad

Boomerangs at La Perouse

Botany Bay from Kurnell

blue bay. A small rock just offshore of the Captain Cook Obelisk is the site of the first recorded white footfall on eastern Australia – that of seaman Isaac Smith.

The National Parks and Wildlife Service maintains **Banks-Solander Track** and the **Discovery Centre** museum (tel: 6689923. Open 10.30 am-4.30 pm Monday-Friday, and 10.30 am-5 pm on weekends and public holidays). A terrific place for easy bushwalks and wide-open space. Spare a thought for the Gwiyagal Aborigines who inhabited this rich area before the arrival of the *Endeavour* and all who followed. Nearby **Towra Point Nature Reserve** is one of the last coastal wetlands in Sydney, providing sanctuary for native and migratory birds. Entry is by National Parks and Wildlife Service permit only.

There is plenty of opportunity to swim at beaches and baths around the bay, from La Perouse to any number of points along the Grand Parade to **Dolls Point** to Kurnell, but beware of sharks, especially in summer. Look for the meshed enclosures. While you're here, you might continue south to **Cronulla**, the city's southernmost and longest surf beach with its 10 kilometres (6 miles) of sand dunes.

4. Darling Harbour

The newest of Sydney's harbourside public areas, the Darling Harbour complex can take as much time as you have. It is easily reached form the city via the monorail. Once there, you can just wander and browse or fill many hours at the Powerhouse Museum ... or the bars.

Memorial at Kurnell

It is difficult to describe Darling Harbour because it has so many facets that each visitor sees it in a different light. And yet, to describe it as a collection of shops, restaurants, bars, museums, funfair, outdoor entertainment and marina, plus a convention centre, a huge exhibition hall, a Chinese garden and an entertainment centre on the fringe of the city does not give it the sense of identity it is quickly developing. On Sunday, when the rest of Sydney has largely shut down, Darling Harbour exudes good spirits and is crowded with locals and visitors alike.

Perhaps the best way to explain Darling Harbour is to put it in a brief historical context. For this is *the* success story of Australian urban renewal. For many years prior to its redevelopment, Darling Harbour fulfilled the role as Sydney's unwashed sink, an industrial eyesore comprising 50 hectares of rail yards, wharfs and factories at Sydney's back door. Then, in 1984, the state premier promised that the area would be "reborn" as a bicentennial gift to the people of Sydney in 1988. It was.

Darling Harbour
400 m / 0.25 miles

The Darling Harbour project was clouded in controversy. One aspect of the development was a monorail between the city and Darling Harbour. Detractors claim that the monorail has destroyed the appearance of the city and still wait for it to be torn down. Others find it a convenient link and willingly front up to pay A$2 per journey. And there is one element of Darling Harbour that didn't happen. Cynical Sydneysiders relate with glee how a proposed casino development is now in permanent limbo because the government couldn't find anyone honest to run it.

Suffice to say that, despite its incomplete state, there is a lot to see and do in Darling Harbour. The shops and bars and restaurants of the **Harbourside Marketplace**, an enormous speciality shopping centre with over 200 outlets, are open from 10 am to 9 pm six days a week and from 10 am to 6 pm on Sundays (tel: 2813999 for information).

The **Exhibition Centre** (tel: 2825000), which has an indoor area without columns the size of five football fields (and all the

Darling Harbour Marketplace

goals are commercial), is the preferred Sydney venue for trade shows from displays of boats or cars to travel products – daily newspapers provide details. Next door, the **Darling Harbour Convention Centre** (tel: 282-5000), a seven-storey spiral edifice that seats up to 3,500 delegates, is the largest in Australia.

There is an appealing concentration of museums and other public entertainment complexes. The **Entertainment Centre** (tel: 2112222, or 11582 for recorded show information) straddles the division between Darling Harbour and Chinatown. Many of the world's greatest stars have trodden the boards of the "Ent Cent" and there looks to be no end to the flow – as long as Sydney's summer coincides with the cold northern winters. Again, newspapers detail forthcoming attractions.

The **Chinese Garden** (tel: 2816863, open from 9.30 am to sunset, admission A$2 adults, A$0.50 children and pensioners) was built as a bicentennial gift by the government of China's Guangdong Province. It is found behind high walls protecting it from the noise pollution of the traffic flow outside. Inside you'll find a peaceful garden refuge of lakes, waterfalls and perfectly executed landscaping.

Tumbalong Park is a grassy circle fringed by eucalypts with tree-lined walks radiating into the middle distance. Catering for playtime for all ages there is both a children's playground and amphitheatre for open air performances. The emphasis in landscaping is on Australian vegetation. Buskers and bands perform here, particularly on sunny weekends.

The **Powerhouse Museum** (open daily from 10 am to 5 pm, tel: 2170111) is now the state's prime tourist attraction. The building started life as the power plant for Sydney's trams and has ended up as a hands-on celebration of arts, technology and social history. It is large enough to contain

Chinese Garden, Darling Harbour

the whole Opera House and there are times when the daunted visitor feels that this edifice must be about the only thing not on display. There is something for everyone – from New South Wales' first passenger train engine, complete with three fitted-out carriages, to crafts and fashion, and a transport section with cars, planes and even a space shuttle. The emphasis is on things Australian, although the international context is not lost. This ongoing exposition by the Museum of Applied Arts and Sciences is a living museum of a people's achievements.

The **Sydney Aquarium** (tel: 2622300, open 9.30 am to 9 pm every day; adults A$12, children and pensioners A$6), on the city side of the cove, and shaped like a breaking wave, contains a good cross-section of the incredible range of fish that inhabit Australian waters. Although there are no crocodiles in New South Wales waters, visitors and locals who are not heading north to the tropics can see them at the aquarium. Sydney certainly does have sharks, however, and nose-to-nose confrontations are reassuringly safe in the aquarium's transparent tunnel surrounded by the inhabitants of the harbour.

The **National Maritime Museum** (tel: 5527777) houses all manner of vessels both as permanent outdoor displays and inside exhibits dealing with all facets of Australians' relationship with the sea. Nearby, **Sydney Seaport** displays an old grain clipper and other lovely old craft. (Tel: 5522011, open daily 10 am-5 pm, adults A$2.)

The venerable **Pier Street Pump House** that provided hydraulic pressure to operate lifts and bank vault doors around the city is now a boutique brewery where you can drink your beer while watching the next one being produced. This tavern is open Monday to Saturday from 11 am to midnight, Sunday 12 noon to 10 pm, and is constantly crowded (tel: 291841).

Pyrmont Bridge, the original road bridge across Darling Harbour, has been retained and provides the fastest pedestrian access to Darling Harbour from the city. The bridge itself, with its quaint control box in the middle, is worthy of inspection. It is an electronically powered "swing span" bridge that pivots horizontally to allow large vessels to enter the inner harbour.

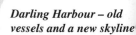

Darling Harbour – old vessels and a new skyline

DAY TRIPS

1. Blue Mountains

Although some of the attractions of the Blue Mountains can be visited by a combination of rail and taxi, the best way to explore this area is by car. The mountains can fill anywhere from a day to a week. However, a full day is sufficient to give you a taste of what the area has to offer.

Seen from any Sydney vantage point, the thin line of the Blue Mountains on the western horizon looks far from impressive. They are not very high. Indeed, **Mount Victoria**, on the Great Western Highway, the highest and coldest point in the range aspires to a mere 1,111 metres (3,645 feet). However, this plateau is so deeply indented that it took 24 years for the first white settlers to find a way across the mountains to the pasture lands of

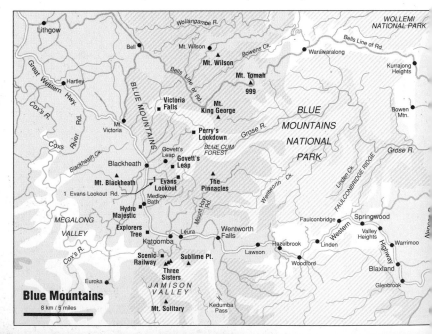

Blue Mountains

8 km / 5 miles

Blue Mountains vista

the west. This results in unusual mountain terrain where most walks involve heading *down* from the road then back *up* to the car at the end of the day.

The Blue Mountains take their name from a trick of the light. Refracted light on minute droplets of eucalyptus oil in the atmosphere from the millions of gum trees which cover the mountains creates a blue haze. The area is part of one of New South Wales' largest national parks and provides surprisingly grand vistas and beautiful gorges and valleys. An added bonus is that when it is hot in Sydney the mountain glens are pleasantly cool. In winter cool temperatures, log fires and the occasional snowfall create a striking contrast to Sydney's temperate days.

In the 1870s the Blue Mountains came to be regarded primarily as a holiday centre – a role they retained for many decades. However, they had fallen out of favour by the 1970s. Since then, there has been a renaissance so that today there are several new resorts, some highly regarded restaurants and eucalyptus forest trails full of healthy walkers.

Katoomba, 100 kilometres (62 miles) west of Sydney, is the major tourist centre of the Blue Mountains and has been a holiday resort for more than a century. It is built on a series of hills that drop steeply into the **Jamison Valley**. The town is well served by electric trains from Sydney (about 90 minutes away) and is on the Great Western Highway. To orientate yourself, go straight to the tourist information centre at **Echo Point** (tel: 047-821-833). A short trail leads to the point that provides a magnificient view past the

The Three Sisters, Katoomba

famous **Three Sisters** rock formation over the Jamison Valley.

The nearby **Giants Stairway** descends by 1,000 steps to the valley floor, from where there are several walks of varying length and difficulty. Treks to the **Ruined Castle** and **Mount Solitary** from here will take most of the day, are fairly hard and require planning. Details of these, and many other walks, are available from the National Parks and Wildlife Service.

One of the easiest walks from the bottom of the stairway is to the right towards the base of the **Scenic Railway.** This enduring tourist attraction has operated safely for many years and was originally constructed in the 1880s to transport miners and coal up from the valley. This is a point to bear in mind as you ascend a seemingly sheer cliff face on the flimsy contraption. Going down is worse: one has the terrifying sensation of plunging vertically 445 metres down to the valley floor (in fact it's a 45 degree incline).

Leura, a town many regard as the prettiest village in the mountains, adjoins Katoomba and is reached by a scenic clifftop drive. Its historic main street has been restored and abounds with craft, antique and tea shops. Visit **Everglades Gardens** with five hectares (12 acres) of landscaped grounds, and **Leuralla** (open 10 am to 5 pm, Friday to Sunday, tel: 047-841169) once the home of Dr H V Evatt – the first president of the United Nations – a stately home built in 1914 in art deco style. The house includes a collection of 19th-century Australian art historical objects and a restaurant. After sightseeing, call in to the luxurious **Fairmont Resort** (tel: 047-825222) poised on the clifftop at Sublime Point, just out of town. This complex is the best accommodation in the mountains – passing travellers can enjoy a drink at the fireside bar or the restaurant with panoramic views across the valley at your feet.

Continuing on the highway along the ridge top westwards from Katoomba, the road passes the **Explorers Tree**, commemorating the successful crossing of the range by Blaxland, Lawson and Wentworth in 1813. For the very adventurous this is also the starting point for the **Six Foot Track**, a bushwalk that takes two to three days and ends at Jenolan Caves. Further on, stop at the **Hydro Majestic Hotel** at **Medlow Bath**. Built between 1880 and 1903, this extraordinary hotel is an Edwardian folly with art deco touches and a cavernous dining room that offers stunning views out over the Megalong Valley.

Blackheath is the next main town along the highway. The local **Rhododendron Garden**, featuring more than 1,500 rhododendrons in a bush setting, is worth a visit, and the area has spectacular views of the tree-lined Grose Valley from **Evans Lookout** and **Govetts Leap**, which are also starting points for several bushwalks into the National Park. The best as an intro-duction to the mountains is the **Grand Canyon walk**, a 3-4 hour hike that is not very tax-ing. Take the signposted road out to Evans Lookout where you leave the car and descend a fairly steep trail into the rain-forest and canyon. The canyon itself is a narrow passage lined with ferns in part then it opens up to a sunny shaded glen. Finally, you climb through a shaded glen to return to the road.

An alternative, more difficult walk is from Perry's Lookdown to the **Blue Gum Forest**. The only hard part of the walk is the descent to the valley floor and the climb out of the valley at the end of the day (either back to Perry's Lookdown or to Govetts Leap). The Blue Gum Forest with its crystal stream, grassy swathes and towering eucalypts is an excellent goal for a day walk. Just save some energy for the climb out.

Lilianfels at Echo Point, near Katoomba, is an 85 room country retreat built around an historic 1890 home. A two acre ornamental garden, bushwalking tracks, stunning views of the Jamison valley and a quality restaurant are among the offerings.

(Tel: 02-2474311) for more information.

From Blackheath, you can also drive down from the escarpment on the other side into the **Megalong Valley**, a tranquil farming area that offers horse riding excursions at the **Packsaddlers** (tel: 047-879150).

On the way back to Sydney call into the **Norman Lindsay Gallery and Museum** at Faulconbridge (open 11 am - 5 pm, Friday to Sunday and on public holidays, tel: 047-511067). Lindsay was one of Australia's most acclaimed and notorious painters, as well as being a writer and sculptor of note. He lived in this stone cottage for 57 years up to his death in 1969. The house contains an important collection of his paintings, drawings, etchings (he specialised in twee scenes of voluptuous Bacchanalia), novels and ship models and is now owned by the National Trust. The landscaped gardens include several of Lindsay's larger statues and fountains.

The only real reason to approach the mountains by the northern road (through **Richmond**, across the Nepean River and along the scenic Bell's Line of Road) is to visit the **Mount Tomah Botanic Garden**. This Bicentennial project is an offshoot of Sydney's Royal Botanic Gardens and displays cool climate plants in a series of walking trails as well as a formal garden. A side excursion from here to **Mount Wilson** is worthwhile because high rainfall and rich volcanic soils have produced some exceptional private gardens which open to the public in spring and autumn. (Check locations and dates on 02-279047 or 047-396266.)

Rail buffs may wish to proceed towards Lithgow, a remarkably unattractive industrial and mining town in a narrow valley. The **Zig Zag Railway** (tel: 063-514826) is located a few kilometres short of Lithgow: it is a 13-kilometre (8-mile) section of rail line ingeniously built in the 1860s to descend the western escarpment of the mountains. The modern line bypassed it, so it was rescued by rail enthusiasts who operate the line at weekends (at 10.30 am, 12.15 pm, 2 pm and 3.30 pm) for tourists to experience a steam train ride and early colonial engineering resourcefulness.

Jenolan Caves

If you have more than a day to spare up in the mountains, just outside Hartley (130 kilometres from Sydney) a turnoff from the Great Western Highway will take you the 48 kilometres (30 miles) to **Jenolan Caves**, long renowned as Australia's most famous limestone cave system.

After passing through **Hampton State Forest**, you skirt the **Kanangra Boyd National Park** along a steep, winding road and eventually round a bend to be confronted by the surprising spectacle of the 24-metre-high **Grand Arch**. The road turns into this gaping cleft in the hillside and emerges outside the Tudor-style sandstone **Jenolan Caves House** (tel: 063-593311). Built at the turn of the century, Caves House has attracted visitors since the caves were first opened to the public. Like much of the mountains facilities, it was looking seedy a few years ago but under new management it has recently been renovated to a high standard of comfort.

According to legend, the caves were first discovered by the white settlers during the pursuit of a bushranger in 1838. Almost 30 years later they were first opened to the public. Now there are six cavern systems open. These caverns contain an amazing diversity of formations – stalactites, stalagmites, paper-thin "straws" and other strangely contorted shapes – all created by the action of air on dripping limestone-bearing water. The entire system forms a massive underground labyrinth of which the readily accessible few are only a tiny portion. Some of the caves can be explored without a guide, others may only be visited as part of a regular tour – you should be wearing sound shoes with good grip and be prepared for quite a lot of walking up and down steps.

Jenolan Caves

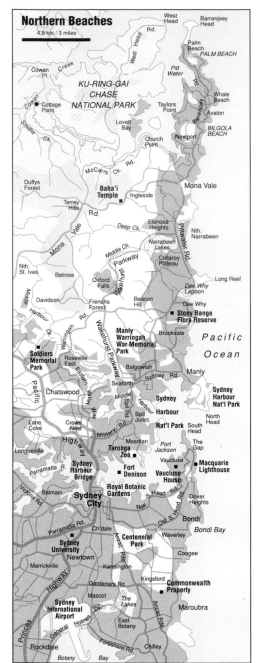

Northern Beaches

4.8 km / 3 miles

KU-RING-GAI CHASE NATIONAL PARK

West Head
Barrenjoey Head
West Head Rd.
Palm Beach
PALM BEACH
Pitt Water
Whale Beach
Cowan Pt.
Cowan Creek
Cottage Point
Taylors Point
Avalon
Lovett Bay
Newport
BILGOLA BEACH
Smiths Ck.
McCarrs Ck. Rd.
Church Point
Duffys Forest
Baha'i Temple
Ingleside
Mona Vale
Terrey Hills Rd.
Elanosa Heights
Nth. Narrabeen
Mona Vale
Deep Ck.
Narrabeen Lakes
Pittwater Rd.
Middle Ck.
Collaroy Plateau
Nth. St. Ives
Belrose
Oxford Falls
Parkway
Wakehurst
Long Reef
Dee Why Lagoon
Davidson
Frenchs Forest
Beacon Hill
Dee Why
Warringah Ck.
Stony Range Flora Reserve
Manly Warringah War Memorial Park
Brookvale
Pacific Ocean
Soldiers Memorial Park
Roseville East
Balgowlah
Wakehurst Parkway
Seaforth
Sydney Rd.
Manly
Chatswood
Eastern Valley Way
Middle Harbour
Sydney
Sydney Harbour Nat'l Park
Spit Rd.
Spit Junct.
North Head
Lane Cove
Crows Nest
Military Rd.
Nat'l Park
South Head
Longueville
Highway
Mosman
Taronga Zoo
Port Jackson
The Gap
Parramatta R.
Sydney Harbour Bridge
Fort Denison
Vaucluse
Macquarie Lighthouse
Balmain
Royal Botanic Gardens
Vaucluse House
Victoria Rd.
Sydney City
S. Head Rd.
Dover Heights
New S. Head Rd.
Ch'dale
Old S. Head Rd.
Bondi
Parramatta Rd.
Centennial Park
Waverley
Bondi Bay
Sydney University
Newtown
Coogee
Marrickville
Kensington
Highway
Gardeners Rd.
Kingsford
Commonwealth Property
Mascot
The Lakes
Maroubra
Sydney International Airport
General Holmes Dr.
Anzac Pde.
East Botany
Princes Highway
Rockdale
Foreshore Rd.
Chifley
Botany
Bay

The finger of land that points north to Palm Beach, bounded by the Pacific Ocean on one side and Pittwater on the other, is the heartland of Sydney's surfing culture. To explore the hedonistic flipside of Sydney's urban lifestyle all you need is a car and a spare day, preferably at the weekend.

From the city, the first part of this journey takes you across the Harbour Bridge, along the boutique shopping strip of Neutral Bay and Mosman's Military Road then across the Spit bridge. Continue to follow the signs to Narrabeen and Palm Beach and a little past Dee Why, 19 kilometres from the city, the road first parallels and gives a view of the Pacific coast. At the end of Dee Why lagoon you'll see **Long Reef Point** and one of the world's most scenic golf courses. Turn right onto Anzac Avenue at the end of the golf course and drive up to the lookout. From this vantage point the coastal topography is immediately apparent. The Sydney coast is a series of headlands dipping inland to form beautiful sheltered beaches then rising to the next point. The houses on these vantage points have panoramic views and comprise some of the city's most desirable real estate.

From here, the suburbs read like a litany from the daily summer surf reports on Sydney radio: Collaroy Beach, Narrabeen Beach, Bungan Beach, Warriewood Beach, Mona Vale Beach, Newport Beach, Bilgola Beach, Avalon Beach, Whale Beach and Palm Beach. Select one that appeals to you and stop for a swim. If there are red and yellow flags up, swim between them or you may end up with a surfboard wedged in your ear. The flagged area will also be patrolled in summer by a lifesaver.

One of the prettiest of the northern beaches is **Bilgola** on the peninsula – turn right at the top of the ridge after Newport and drive down to the car park. This is the location of a small community snuggled into the diminutive cove far below Barrenjoey Road.

Continuing on to **Palm Beach**, the peninsula flattens out before rising to Barrenjoey ("baby kangaroo") lighthouse, picturesquely perched 113 metres above the waters of Broken Bay at the very tip of the peninsula. Palm Beach is the favoured address of media personalities, film industry folk and anyone else who doesn't have to drive into the city every day.

By now it should be lunchtime. There are a number of options here. To really drop into the spirit of things you should buy (at Newport, Avalon or Palm Beach) some prawns or fish and chips wrapped in newspaper and eat them on a beach.

There are several good restaurants at Palm Beach. **Barrenjoey House** (1108 Barrenjoey Road, tel: 9744001) is expensive but its Australian/French food is almost as good as its setting. However, Sydney's foodies recommend nearby **Beach Road Restaurant** (1 Beach Road, tel: 9141159) as a good combination of reasonable prices, great location and excellent food.

There is yet another option, one which qualifies as a Sydney

Palm Beach and Barrenjoey Headland

Northern Beaches panorama

institution. Retrace your steps to the **Newport Arms** (Kalinya Street, Newport, tel: 9974900) on Pittwater which is a legendary northside hotel. Although there are cheaper places to buy lunch and much easier places to find parking, a pub lunch in the beer garden of the Newport Arms during summer is a chance to drop straight into Sydney's surfing and sailing cultures.

To return to the city, drive south to Mona Vale, then take Mona Vale Road running along the coastal highlands. Set high in the bushland and commanding a spectacular view four kilometres from the coast is the imposingly exotic **Baha'i Temple** at Ingleside that is open to the public. If you have time, turn into McCarr's Creek Road and then into **Ku-ring-gai National Park** and along to **West Head**. This park of 14,712 hectares (36,339 acres) was dedicated in 1894 to preserve an example of Sydney's original landscape. With luck you may see a koala here. In any case, the views over Pittwater from the **West Head** lookout are worth the detour. There are many walking trails in the park, ranging from short strolls to full day outings to secluded beaches. If you wish to take to the water rather than merely overlook it, there are boat hiring facilities at **Akuna Bay** and **Bobbin Head**.

Return to Mona Vale Road, turn right and follow the signs to the Pacific Highway (about 20 minutes), then turn left on the Highway and head to the city (about 30 minutes). This takes you through a cross-section of the affluent northern suburbs (known collectively and misleadingly as "the North Shore") whose descriptions are invariably prefixed with the adjective "leafy". It's not hard to see why.

3. Hawkesbury River Cruise

Take a day trip to the Hawkesbury River to the north of Sydney. The suburbs don't reach this far – but you can join the last Australian riverboat run, dropping supplies to isolated communities.

Although **Brooklyn** is less than an hour by car from Sydney, the best way to get there is by train. Stepping on the air-conditioned inter-city train at Central Railway and stepping off only a short walk from the riverboat wharf certainly beats fighting against the northern suburbs' morning traffic. At main stations like Central you can buy a combined rail and mailboat ticket – it's no cheaper, just more convenient.

There was a time when much of Australia's mail was carried by river transport. However, the development of road and rail has reduced that flow to a single trickle: the **Hawkesbury Riverboat Postman**. There are several small communities along the Hawkesbury that are only accessible by water, others use boats to eliminate a long, circuitous drive. Letters are not all that the little mail boat carries: it delivers everything from milk and groceries to building supplies.

The Riverboat Mail Run departs Brooklyn at 9.30 am each weekday (except public holidays) and returns around 1.15 pm. On Wednesday and Friday it also completes an afternoon run, leaving at 1.30 am and returning about 4.15 pm. To allow plenty of time, you should catch the 8.09 am train from Central Railway. A smorgasbord lunch is available for A$12 on board the boat or you can wait for lunch at one of the cafes or hotel at Brooklyn upon your

Baha'i Temple, Ingleside

return. The fare of A$18 includes morning or afternoon tea. It's a good idea to book the cruise in advance a day or so – tel: 9857566.

Apart from the oddity value of participating in an aquatic mail run, this trip is a good way to see one of the most attractive areas of bushland in the Sydney region. Much of the area remains heavily forested with eucalypts while the characteristic crags of Hawkesbury River sandstone tower overhead.

Of course, the mail run is not the only way to experience the Hawkesbury. If you have the time, drive or catch the train to Brooklyn, then hire an outboard powered dinghy. This promises a day of great scenery on safe water, plus a little fishing if you like. Try **Dori's Boats** or **Baymac Marina**. A small boat costs about A$50 per day.

Another option is to hire a yacht or houseboat and to explore the river over several days. Some 20 charter outlets operate from Pittwater (Newport, Bayview and Church Point), Brooklyn, Bobbin Head, Akuna Bay and, much further upstream, from Wisemans Ferry. Boats range from yachts of all varieties to motor cruisers and houseboats. Some recommended operators are **Skipper a Clipper** (tel: 4501888), **Hawkesbury Water Ways Hire Cruisers** (tel: 4562866) and the long-established **Halvorsens** (tel: 4579011) for motor cruisers, **Pittwater Yacht Charters** (tel: 9975344) for sailing craft and **Fenwicks Marina** (tel: 985 7633)

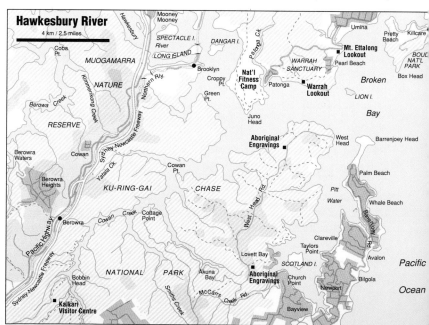

Hawkesbury River Bridge, Brooklyn

for the flat-bottomed variety.

You don't have to take to the water at all to see the Hawkesbury. Much of this deep, sheltered waterway is bounded by national parks – coastal Bouddi and Brisbane Waters, the rugged wilderness of Dharug, Marramarra and Ku-ring-gai Chase. Camping is permitted in most of the five national parks, but conditions vary from basic bush camping to fully-equipped sites. It is best to check with the National Parks and Wildlife Service office in Cadman's Cottage, 110 George Street, Sydney, tel: 278861.

4. Royal National Park

The **Royal National Park** at Sutherland on the southern limits of Sydney had a historical role of global significance. It was created in 1879 and is the second oldest public reserve in the world only Yellowstone in the United States (formed in 1872) is older. However, the Royal was the world's first "national park" (a title that was also subsequently given to Yellowstone, in 1883). The Sydney park later had a name change –

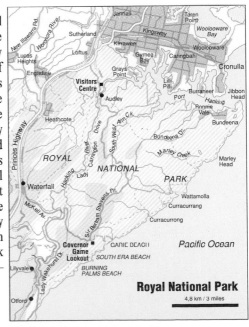

the "Royal" tag was bestowed by Queen Elizabeth during a visit to Sydney in 1954.

With the establishment of this and Yellowstone, the concept of natural areas set aside for public use was born. However, the idea of preserving native bush was far from the thoughts of the park's founders. While national parks are today regarded as areas where the environment is preserved in perpetuity, this park was intended as a pleasure ground to be modelled after London's Hampstead Heath. Some of the Australian bush was torn out to be replaced by imported plants and manicured lawns. Until 1922 the trust for this 15,000-hectare region earned an income from logging. Rabbits and foxes were introduced, and Javanese rusa deer and fallow deer released into the park around the end of last century are still there.

Although the park still lacks a feeling of pristine wilderness in the most well-frequented areas, several regions of attractive bushland can be found by anyone prepared to walk. Bounded by Port Hacking to the north, the Pacific Ocean to the east and the railway line to the west, the Royal is predominantly heath-covered sandstone plateau. However, the valleys are full of rainforests, with a luminous green luxuriance of buttress roots, liana vines and innumerable ferns. The native animals are timid and most are nocturnal so visitors don't see them with the same frequency as the 200 bird types in the park.

Within the park's dense grottoes one may hear a whip bird (its call sounds like a stock whip being cracked) or see the exquisite lyre bird, named for its lyre-shaped tail. Look out for the satin bower bird: it looks like a raven at first glance but a closer look reveals that the bird's plumage is a deep irridescent mauve.

The Royal National Park is easy to reach from Sydney by road or public transport. If driving, just follow the Princes Highway to the turnoff into the park at Loftus. The alternatives for train travellers are to travel along the Illawarra line and disembark at one of the several stations around or within the park (Waterfall, Helensburg or Otford) then walk in. Or you can take a train to Cronulla and take a ferry across Port Hacking to Bundeena.

The main visitor centre and wildlife shop (open 9 am–4 pm, tel: 5420648) is at **Audley**. This has a lot of information about the park. Or you can obtain some brochures in advance from the National Parks and Wildlife Service office in Cadman's Cottage, 110 George Street, Sydney, tel: 278861.

There are over 150 kilometres (154 miles) of walking trails and numerous picnic and barbecue facilities within the park. You can rent canoes or paddleboats at Audley.

The roads through the Royal are not just day access routes: several are roads between the south coast and Sydney (although the Princes Highway to Wollongong skirts the park's western boundary), and the Bundeena Road provides the only road access to that fishing village. **Lady Carrington Drive** that follows the Hacking River valley is flat, wide and closed to traffic, so it's good for cycling and walking.

Along the shores of the park there are 24 kilometres of coastline: surfing beaches interspersed by rugged sandstone headlands. **Era, Burning Palms** and **Garie beaches** are the most popular surfing beaches and **Bundeena** is a renowned windsurfing area. The well-appointed camping area of **Bonnie Vale** nearby is adjacent to a sandy spot which is good for swimming. **Wattamolla** has a good swimming lagoon and attracts many snorkellers and divers keen to explore the inlet.

Royal National Park

Shopping

There's much more to shopping in Sydney than opals and boomerangs. The only limits are your budget and excess baggage allowance. The following shopping spree covers a range of consumptions, but stops short of that favourite export of many Japanese tourists, freezer packs of prime Aussie beef.

"**Australiana**" covers a multitude of sins and skins. Americans (who have enough beef at home) tend to stock up on **Akubra felt hats** and **Driza Bone oilskin coats** for the "Man from Snowy River" look, while, with all that frozen beef, the Japanese departure is more like the "Man from Snowy Liver". Many stores stock Australian rural gear, but the most famous is **R M Williams** (389 George Street), because the old living legend, "R M" himself, designed, wears and still manufactures much of it. However, if you're looking for a bargain in Driza Bone drovers' coats, at the mouth of King's Cross subway station (in Darlinghurst Road), a little hole-in-the-wall place sells them about 20 percent cheaper than the "bush boutiques". **Thomas Cook Boot & Clothing** (709 George Street) carries a large range of High Country gear. Less macho garments can be found at various **Ken Done** shops (Darling Harbour, Skygarden, The Rocks), or sheepskin products at **Aries** (273 George Street).

Non-wearable Australiana and de-kitsched souvenirs can be purchased at gift shops in the **Australian Museum** (corner of William and College streets), the **Botanical Gardens**, the **Art Gallery of New South Wales**, the **Opera House**, and National Trust historic buildings like **Juniper Hall** (248 Oxford Street, Paddington). The **Wattle Tree Shop** (294 Oxford Street) carries all-Australian trinkets, toys, clothes, and jewellery.

"Oztraliana" can range from feral kitsch (kangaroo and sheep doorstops) to utilitarian items (stationery, household gadgets) to unbearably fluffy koalas (made in Taiwan), fur purses, boomerangs and T-shirts. Of the sheepskin items, lambskin underlays for beds and cots are the best buys.

Popular tourist shopping beats are **The Rocks**, **Chinatown**, **Darling Harbour** (Harbourside Festival Marketplace) and **Birkenhead Point** (at Drummoyne). The Central Business District area bounded by Hunter, Park, Clarence and Elizabeth streets sees most of the retail and duty-free shopping action by Sydneysiders. It contains, among others, **Centrepoint**, the **Imperial Arcade**, **Mid-City Complex**, **Strand Arcade**, **Skygarden** and **Queen Victoria Building**. All of these house scores of speciality gift, clothing, book, music, jewellery and craft and art shops. Beyond the city area, those suburbs renowned for power purchasing include **Mosman**, **Neutral Bay** and **Chatswood** (all north of the Bridge) and **Paddington**, **Bondi Junction** and **Double Bay** to the east of the city. **Remo General Store** (corner of Oxford and Crown streets, Darlinghurst) specialises in quality gifts, clothing and furnishings. **Sax Leather** (110A Oxford Street) has very good sandals and belts.

Some city pointers are: **Flamingo Park** in the Strand Arcade, the home of Jenny Kee's distinctly Australian hand-knit designs in

Skygarden on Pitt Street Mall

sweaters, skirts, shirts and scarves. **Ken Done** is an Australian designer whose art is wearable and ubiquitous: his shops sell everything from sweatshirts and beachwear to placemats, linen and umbrellas. **Skygarden** (77 Castlereagh Street) is as light and elevated as its name suggests. Six floors of parquetry, boutiquery, taste, tiles, "name"

apparel and galleries.

The **"Golden Square"** corner of King, Castlereagh and Elizabeth streets packs in a little ghetto of excellence: Celine, Lowe and Louis Vuitton, etc, at their elegant best. Close by is Sydney's favourite department store, **David Jones** (known universally as "DJs"), billed as "the most beautiful store in the world". There are two DJs emporia, at Elizabeth Street and Market Street, the former the more elegant, the latter with a scrumptious basement Food Hall.

Retail trading hours in Sydney are generally 9 am to 5.30 pm, Monday to Friday, and until 9 pm on Thursday evenings, with varied hours on Saturday afternoon. Sunday is generally comatose. Darling Harbour Marketplace is open until 9 pm every night. Some bookshops (eg **Ariel** at 42 Oxford Street, Paddington) are open till late, and sometimes all weekend. **Chinatown** shops are open daily from 8.30 am to 6 pm, if not later.

For market bargains and fun, the **Paddington Village Bazaar**, held on Saturdays in the Uniting Church in Oxford Street, is a rainbow mix of people and products: genuine home-made crafts, the works of young fashion designers, jewellers and artists, second-hand clothes, books and collectables.

Opals: Many jewellery shops in the central shopping district (particularly in Pitt and Castlereagh streets) sell prized Australian opals and sapphires, either set or loose. Look for "black" opals (with deeper colours, green and blue, nearly always sold as a thin wafer of opal between a dark backing and a transparent cap) and "white" opals (a light background shot through with colours, normally sold as a solid stone). **Michal's** of Double Bay (also in David Jones Elizabeth Street store), **Opal Skymine** (Australia Square Tower, George Street, near Wynyard Station), **Rocks Opal**

Mine (Clocktower Square, The Rocks), **E Gregory Sherman**, **Flame Opals**, **Skippy Opals** and **Gemtec** in the city are but a few.

Good opals are not cheap, but there is plenty of competition, so compare products and prices. If you find a purchase (of opals or anything else) is faulty, take it back for exchange or refund (always keep your receipts). New South Wales has clear consumer protection laws, and if you experience difficulties with the vendor, call the Department of Business and Consumer Affairs on 2668911.

Aboriginal Art: Bark paintings are the most common form of Koori (Aboriginal) art, but also consider contemporary works on board, or carved boomerangs and didgeridoos. Prices for paintings can range from A$100 to many thousands. Try the **Aboriginal Art Centre**, 7 Walker Lane, Paddington, or in The Rocks at the Argyle Centre and the Clock Tower Building. The **Aboriginal Artists' Gallery** is at 477 Kent Street and at the Opera House. **Coo-ee Aboriginal Art Gallery** is said to stock Australia's largest selection of Aboriginal arts and crafts. There are shops at Oxford Street, Paddington (Nos 202 and 98), and at 88 George Street, The Rocks.

Food: Beside slabs of frozen beef, local delicacies include macadamia nuts, bush honey, bee pollen and royal jelly, chocolates and the inevitable Vegemite, a savoury spread made of yeast extract. One shop which carries a good range is **Milagold** underneath the Hyatt Kingsgate Hotel, King's Cross. Australian wines can be purchased at any pub or bottle shop, with fair quality wines starting at about A$10 per bottle. The flag bearer of Australian wines is an exquisite albeit expensive red: Penfolds Grange Hermitage.

Duty-Free Goods: Purchasing duty-free goods is simple: just bring your passport and onward ticket. Numerous duty-free shops are located along Pitt Street, south from the Ramada Renaissance Hotel – check in the yellow pages for the full gauntlet.

Paddington Bazaar for the unexpected

There has been a remarkable change in Sydney, and indeed Australia, over the past decade or so. It has gone from being a gastronomical desert (with a single "s") to one of the world's culinary innovators. Much of the credit for this must rest with the waves of immigrants that have flowed into the country, bringing their national cuisines – and respect for the art of food preparation – with them. Australia, with its selection of fruit and vegetables from tropical to temperate and excellent farm produce has always had excellent ingredients. It now cooks them well, too.

To experience the best in Australian cuisine, one that straddles the globe from Lyon to Bangkok, with passing acknowledgement to Rome and Peking, you should visit at least one of Sydney's top restaurants. Expect the food to be exemplary, the service less so. Also on the downside are the rapid rises and falls that characterise Sydney restaurants: by the time you read this, the scene will have changed. Even so, the restaurants selected here have established some continuity and look set to continue at the same standards. We hope.

The best restaurant in Sydney (and perhaps Australia) has long been **Berowra Waters Inn** (open for lunch and dinner on Friday and Saturday, lunch only on Sunday, tel: 4561027). Getting there is an excursion – it's on an inlet of the Hawkesbury River, well north of the city. The most convenient approach is also the most expensive – by floatplane from Rose Bay – but it is also accessible by road (about 40 minutes drive) and a short boat transfer. In any case, it's worth the effort: the setting is magnificent and Gay Bilson, your hostess, is a genius. At A$80 per person plus wine, the meal is a fraction of the price of equivalent meals in France. The service here is almost the equal of the food.

However, you don't have to go this far for a very good Sydney meal. **Claude's** (at Woollahra, open for dinner Tuesday-Saturday, tel: 331-2325) is an excellent French restaurant in the Eastern Suburbs. It's only small and is BYO – bring-your-own (bottle of whatever) – but there is nothing offhand about the quality of the food or service. Claude's is a venue for serious dining – eat and enjoy it.

Paddington's **Oasis Seros** (open for dinner Tuesday-Saturday, tel: 3613377) is at the cutting edge of innovative Australian cuisine. The decor may appear antique-minimalist and some of the dishes unfamiliar but any discussion of the best Australian chefs will inevitably include Phillip Searle, the proprietor of Oasis Seros.

It is unfortunate that a good new restaurant instantly becomes trendy – and stays that way until the next one opens. Down in The

Hard Rock Cafe, Crown Street

Rocks, Neil Perry's **Rockpool** (open for lunch and dinner Monday-Saturday, tel: 2521888) is, as the name suggests, a seafood restaurant. It's the best place in Sydney to see how good Australia's ocean bounty can be when well prepared. If the "foodies" have moved on by the time you arrive, consider yourself lucky. If you're budgetting, try the Rockpool's **Oyster Bar**.

Many world-weary travellers claim that there are three types of restaurant meals – good ones, bad ones and hotel meals. Anyone who has had the good fortune to dine in any of the world's great hotel restaurants will find this statement remarkably inaccurate. To disprove it entirely, dine at **The Point** (open for lunch and dinner Monday to Friday, dinner only on Saturday, tel: 3683000) the Australian/French restaurant in the new Nikko Hotel near

King's Cross. The imported chefs here have a galaxy of Michelin stars to their credit – and they are clearly revelling in Australian ingredients and the chance to develop new dishes. Meals here are both satisfying and innovative and service is good.

Spoons with a View: If you regard a meal as requiring more than food alone, there are many Sydney restaurants that provide a spoon with a view. With the exception of Berowra Waters Inn, none provides great cuisine, but who will notice when confronted with panoramas like these have? Some of these restaurants have already been covered in the chapters on their areas (such as the **Bennelong** at the Opera House and **Le Kiosk** and **Faulty Bowers** at Manly).

By dint of hard promotion over many years, **Doyles on the Beach** (open for lunch and dinner seven days, tel: 3372007) has become a Sydney institution. There is no disputing the glorious setting – you look straight down the harbour to the bridge – but it is a very expensive fish-and-chip restaurant. A much cheaper alternative is the beer garden of the **Watsons Bay Hotel** (tel: 3374299) next door.

Most of Sydney's picturesque restaurants are on the waterfront. The **Bathers Pavilion** (open for lunch and dinner seven days, tel: 9681133) has a great location overlooking Balmoral Beach: ask for a window table. After the meal, a promenade along the beautiful waterfront can develop into a love affair with Sydney. Further north of town, **Freshwater Restaurant** (open lunch and dinner seven days, tel: 9385575) on Harbord Beach (also known sometimes as Freshwater Beach) is a beautiful spot on a sunny day. Food and service are both good and the daytime views energising.

There are a couple of very upmarket restaurants around The Rocks' waterside. **Bilsons** at the International Passenger Terminal (open for lunch and dinner Monday-Friday, dinner only Saturday and Sunday, tel: 2515600) and **No 7 at the Park** (in the Park Hyatt Hotel, open for lunch and dinner seven days, tel: 2561630) are both expensive and one suspects this is largely a viewpoint surcharge.

On the western side of the bridge and on the northern side of the harbour stands **Sails Harbourside** (open for lunch and dinner Monday to Saturday, lunch only on Sunday, tel: 9555793) at Mc-Mahons Point. Meals and service can both be erratic but the view across the water to the city is exceptional.

Also on the "wrong" side of the bridge but this time on the city side of the harbour is the **Wharf** restaurant (at the end of Pier 4, Walsh Bay, open for lunch and dinner Monday to Satur-day, tel: 2501761). The food is very good, the setting superb (especially on the outside deck in summer) and the prices moderate. It is not plush but provides one of Sydney's best waterside

dining experiences. It is also adjacent to the foyer of the Wharf Theatre, so consider combining dining with some good Sydney Theatre Company drama or comedy.

Although you won't find it in many guide books, there is another restaurant overlooking the harbour that is worth a visit. The **Indian Empire** (5 Walker Street, North Sydney, tel: 9232909) is an unpretentious Indian eatery that just happens to have spectacular views over the harbour. It is a much cheaper venue than the others mentioned but the food is good (by Sydney Indian restaurant standards) and the service is down-home friendly.

Of course, Sydney does not escape the rooftop eyrie, revolving tower restaurant – aka "pie-in-the-sky" dining. The **Summit** (open for lunch and dinner seven days, tel: 2479777) is on top of Australian Square – the food and service are fair but you are really paying for the view. Expect this, the world's largest revolving restaurant, to be filled with flocks of tourists. You have a choice of **Sydney Tower Restaurants** (open for lunch and dinner seven days, tel: 2333722) at the top of the tower above Centrepoint: an *à la carte* or self service. Accept that the view is more important than the food here and choose the cheaper self service venue – once there, aim for the plainer fare that is very well cooked in a lunch-at-mum's style.

Despite justifiable reservations about the quality of the cuisine, every visitor to Sydney should visit one of these high-altitude restaurants once. From this vantage point high above the city, Sydney's unique topography is laid out like a 3-D road map. From here you can watch aircraft land at Mascot, boats sail the harbour and look to the Blue Mountains. By the end of the meal, the layout of the city will make sense for the first time.

Without a clearly defined Australian cuisine, Sydney has developed what may be the world's best array of international cuisines within a single city. Forty pages of restaurant listings in the Yellow Pages directory include a "cuisine guide" with 35 headings from African to Vietnamese. For the past few years, Thai has definitely been the flavour in favour. Among the best of the genre are the **Bangkok** (tel: 361 4804) in East Sydney, **Darley Street Thai** (tel: 550 6650) in Newton, and **Prasit's** on Crown (tel: 331 3026) in Darlinghurst.

Sydney excels in the number of cheap eateries throughout the city and suburbs that serve good meals from every cuisine in the world. It is beyond the scope of this book to cover the many thousands of offerings: the gourmet gospel is the *Good Food Guide* published annually by the *Sydney Morning Herald*. The alternative is *Cheap Eats in Sydney*, available at any newsagent for A$6.95. *Bon appetit.*

Nightlife

Kings Cross Hotel

"The night is young" takes on literal meaning in some Sydney scenes, as if there were invisible age barriers (and very visible fashion barriers) to mixing. In some of the clubs and rock pubs you won't feel too comfortable if you are over 30 – or in other places if you are under 30.

Singles (gay and straight) and couples are welcome at most of the following places. In Sydney, the definition of a woman's night on the town is not necessarily "dances with wolves"; single women are pestered no more than in comparable countries – that is, still too often for their liking. Dress codes vary, from *de rigueur* designer fashion to "neat casual", but sloppy or dirty clothing will often keep you out on the street. If you look young, you must have identification to prove that you are over 18 (the minimum legal drinking age). For up-to-the-moment listings, consult Friday's *Sydney Morning Herald* entertainment supplement, "Metro", or giveaway music papers like *Culture, Drum Media, OTS* and *3-D*.

Clubs and Discos: Like their own butterfly clientele, some nightclubs have a brief, intense lifespan, and may not be there, at least by the same name, next time you look. The action heats up

Harry's Cafe de Wheels

after 10.30 pm, although many clubs have good restaurant facilities for earlier dining. Cover charges vary from zero to A$10 and upwards, depending upon who/what you are/know, how you dress, the night of the week – and the whim of the door prefect. Opening times vary. Call first for accurate info.

Try the following:

Black Market Cafe (111 Regent Street, Chippendale, tel: 6988863) has a very good downstairs restaurant, *fin-de-siècle* post mod design, and, upstairs, a booming dance floor and pool tables. Less pretentious than many inner-city clubs, **Kinsela's** (Bourke and Campbell Streets, Taylor Square, tel: 331 6200) has food, booze and boom. Deco decor, "style sergeants" on the door. It used to be a funeral parlour, and people in black are still dying to get in. **Kings Cross Hotel** (William and Victoria Streets, King's Cross, tel: 3583377) is loud and crowded on the weekend, full of young suburbanites come to town for the night and the thrill.

Hard Rock Cafe (121 Crown Street, Darlinghurst, tel: 3311116) is cloned from namesakes in too many other countries. Rock litter (Elvis' mink hernia belt and false teeth) adorns the bar. More glamorous door queues (just like a bus stop), but good burgers and huge servings – though conversation gets decibelled to death. Speak braille. **Studebakers** (19 Bayswater Road, King's Cross, tel: 3585656) is another chain clone. Big, bright, new, groovy for tourists and locals. Buffet included in entrance fee. Catch the bright red 1951 Bulletnose Studey in the foyer, a classic. **The Cauldron** (207 Darlinghurst Road, King's Cross, tel: 3311523) is packed with a largely single, horny, professional crowd, and its tiny dance floor guarantees a lot of personal contact. Good food too. Major hotels have their own clubs, such as **Juliana's** at the Sydney Hilton (259 Pitt Street) and **William's**

at the Sydney Boulevard (90 William Street).

The Freezer (11 Oxford Street, Paddington, tel: 3322568) has an upstairs restaurant and cocktail bar and downstairs disco. What was saved on decor (elaborate, like an icebox) may have been spent on a brick bungalow in the suburbs. Cool clientele is at one with all this. **The Site** (171 Victoria Street, King's Cross, tel: 3586511) is next door to the popular Soho Bar. Dress sharp for the industrial wasteland decor. Models, fashion editors and other Nutrasweets welcome. **Bobby McGee's** (377 Harbourside Festival Marketplace, Darling Harbour, tel: 2813944) is a fine, roaring joint in which to be young and in lust, or even a little older and in love. Beer, loud music, the crush of bodies, water views. Other dance clubs include **Base**, **Mars** and **The Tunnel**.

Pub Rock: Social stratification by doorperson is less prevalent in rock pubs. All major live rock venues can be found listed in the Friday *Sydney Morning Herald* "Metro" section. The **Tom Tom Club** (22 Bayswater Road, King's Cross, tel: 3585228) open late and live, seven nights. **Lucy's Tavern** (54 Castlereagh Street, tel: 2314738) attracts an office crowd as the weekend approaches the music and clientele get louder. **St James Underground Tavern** (80 Castlereagh Street, tel: 221-2460) is good for after work

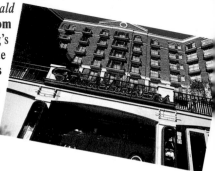

Studebakers club, Kings Cross

drinks with the office crowd and weekend rabble-rousers. The **Woolloomoolo Bay Hotel** (2 Bourke Street, Woolloomooloo, tel: 3571928) has live bands, retro music, good crowds throughout the weekend, and is popular day and night. The **Richmond Riverboat** (tel: 247 2979) departs from Pier One, Walsh Bay, at 7.30 pm on Friday and Saturday nights. Offers a combination of live music/disco and dinner cruises on the harbour.

Jazz: There is a healthy jazz scene, both traditional and contemporary, ranging from the **Don Burrows Supper Club** in the Regent Hotel and the **Jazz Room** of the Inter-Continental Hotel, through the following:

Real Ale Cafe (66 King Street, City, tel: 2623277) has great food, drink and music. Live jazz, seven nights a week. The **Richmond Riverboat** (tel: 2472979) has a jazz cruise on Sunday from 12 noon to 4 pm, departing from Pier One, Hickson Road, Walsh Bay. Top jazz and blackboard menu. **Round Midnight** (2 Roslyn Street, King's Cross, tel: 3564045) is good for late-night jazz and blues. Comfortable ambience. As the name says, not much happening until after 11 pm. Both **Soup Plus** (383 George Street, tel: 297728) and the **Harbourside Brasserie** (Pier One,

The Opera House

Hickson Road, The Rocks, tel: 2523000) are sane, smokey places, quality jazz oriented, and serving more than passable fare.

Caffeine Culture: Adjacent to King's Cross is Darlinghurst ("Darlo"/"Darling-it-hurts"/"Darling-hearse"), the place for heart-starter coffee. Along Victoria Street (heading south, away from the mêlée of the Cross), **Andiamo, Formula One, Tropicana, Morgans, Nicolina's, Back Door, Bar Coluzzi, Unas** and TJs, along with **Michaelangelo's** (corner of William and Darlinghurst Streets) and the 24-hour **Cafe Hernandez** (60 King's Cross Road), all serve coffee of great conviction, and most also serve light meals. Ten minutes walk west, down towards the Central Business District, in Stanley Street (between Crown and Riley Streets) in East Sydney, more cafes (such as **Bill and Tony's**) offer the same Italianate acceleration and pasta ballast.

Live Theatre, Concerts, Ballets, Operas: These also thrive in Sydney. Check the listings in the "Metro" section of Saturday's *Herald* or the *Telegraph Mirror* for details. The **"Halftix"** booth in Martin Place sells reduced-price tickets for many performances (but only if bought in person, in cash, for that evening's performance). Open Monday-Saturday, 12 noon-6 pm.

Movies: The big first-release cinemas are located in George Street (between Bathurst and Liverpool Streets) and in Pitt Street (between Market and Park Streets). Visit the **State Theatre** at 49 Market Street for its sumptuous art deco interior. Again, check the "Metro" section or Saturday's *Herald* to find out what's on. The **Valhalla** (Glebe), **Academy Twin** (Paddington), **Dendy** (Martin Place) and **Village** (Double Bay) tend to quality films (rather than *Mutant Poltergeist Terminators 3*), while the **Hayden Orpheum** (Cremorne) is a restored gem of 1920s "picture palace" architecture.

Finally, for a quirky midnight snack (anyone for coffee with a meat pie chaser?), check the famous **Harry's Cafe de Wheels** on the Woolloomooloo waterfront at Cowper Wharf Road. It's the caravan up on the pavement, surrounded by nighthawks and cabs parked on the traffic island. It accepts no known credit cards.

Calendar of Special Events

School Holidays in New South Wales

Transport reservations and hotel bookings are very heavy during these holidays, so book well in advance. Christmas through until the end of January is summer holiday season for many workers and all students. Be prepared for plenty of company everywhere, and for pretty slow business responses.

Christmas/Summer: mid-December to end of January.

Easter: 10 days over Easter.

Winter: Last week in June to second week in July.

Spring: Last week in September to second week in October.

Cultural and Sporting Diary

26 January: Australia Day
January–February: Festival of Sydney
February: Chinese New Year
February: Gay Mardi Gras Parade
March: Royal Easter Show
March: Golden Slipper (horse racing)
April: Heritage Week
April: Sydney Cup (horse racing)
April: Coca Cola Surfing Classic
April: Dragon Boat Festival at Darling Harbour

June: Australian Art Biennale (even years)
June: Ski Season opens
April: Sydney Film Festival
August: City-to-Surf Race
August: Start of Around Australia Yacht Race
September: Rugby League and Rugby Union Grand Finals
October: Bathurst 1000 saloon car race
October: Bowral Tulip Festival
October: Upper Hunter Wine Festival
October: Opera House Open Day and Pageant
December: Carols by Candlelight
26 December: Start of Sydney-to-Hobart Yacht Race

Practical Information

TRAVEL ESSENTIALS

When to Visit

Any time is fine, though obviously summer (December-February) is hotter, and winter (June-August) is colder and windier. (The seasons are the opposite of those found in the Northern Hemisphere.) Spring (September-November) and autumn (March-May) are delightful times, usually with clear skies. There are no "must see" annual events (like Carnivale in Rio or springtime in the Rockies) which impel one to visit at a specific time.

Visas

All visitors require a passport and visa to enter Australia, except for New Zealanders, who require a passport only. Visas are free and valid for up to six months. Application is made to your nearest Australian or British government representative. An onward or return ticket and sufficient funds are required.

To extend your stay, contact the Department of Immigration one month before your visa expires. Again you will have to show sufficient funds and an onward ticket. The maximum time, including extensions, allowed to visitors

is one year. Check in the front of the telephone book under Immigration Department. The head office is 190 George Street, Sydney, tel: 2584555.

Customs Regulations

Visitors 18 years old and over can bring in duty free 250 cigarettes or 250 gm tobacco or cigars, one litre of alcoholic liquor and other dutiable goods are allowed in the personal baggage of children under the age of 18. Sydney (Kingsford Smith) Airport has an inbound duty-free shop.

Australia has very strict regulations on the importation of foods, plants animals and their by-products. Assume that almost anything of this nature will be confiscated at Customs. Heavy jail penalties apply to drug smuggling of *any* kind.

Australia is rabies-free and all incoming animals are placed in quarantine. Minimum periods for cats and dogs – including seeing-eye dogs – are six months. No exceptions.

Vaccinations

Vaccinations are not required if you are flying directly to Australia and have not been in a smallpox-, yellow fever-, cholera- or typhoid-infected area in the 14 days prior to arrival.

How to Get There

Sydney is Australia's major international gateway, with flights from Asia, the Pacific, Europe, Africa and North America. Some 23 international airlines have regular scheduled flights to Sydney.

Money Matters

Australia's currency is the Australian dollar. Coins come in 5-, 10-, 20- and 50-cent, $1 and $2 denominations. Notes are $5, $10, $50 and $100. You may bring in or take out a maximum of A$5,000 (or its equivalent in foreign currency) in cash.

Foreign Exchange

Most foreign currencies can be cashed at the airport. City banks will exchange currencies between 9.30 am and 5 pm Friday. International-class hotels will change major currencies for guests. There are bureaux de change in some major tourist areas (The Rocks, Kings Cross, the Central Business District), but these are not found elsewhere, so it is best to arrange your foreign exchange before an outing.

At the time of writing A$1 buys (approximately): US$0.78, C$0.91, NZ$1.31, British £0.47. German DM1.48, French F5.04, Japanese ¥107.

Credit Cards

The most widely accepted cards are American Express, Diners Club, Mastercard and Visa. In small establishments you may encounter difficulties with lesser known overseas cards. With any card problems, call:

American Express: 2390666
Diners Club: 2368923
Mastercard: (008) 022017
Visa: 9576133

Travellers' Cheques

All well-known international travellers' cheques can be readily cashed at airports, banks, hotels, motels and similar establishments. Offices of Thomas Cook and American Express are in the city centre. Encashment fees and rates of exchange vary between establishments.

Clothing

For a summer visit include a sweater or jacket to cope with the occasional cool spell. Also bring or buy an umbrella. Don't forget your swimming costume and sunglasses. A sunhat will provide protection against the Australian sun, and a pair of good walking shoes is recommended. In spring and autumn, clothing should be light to medium weight. During winter include warm clothing, a raincoat and umbrella – though it never snows in Sydney, and rarely gets below about 10 degrees centigrade (50 degrees Fahrenheit), it can *feel* really chilly. In general, Australians are casual dressers, and lightweight comfortable clothes are ideal for Sydney. For dining at better hotels and restaurants, a jacket and tie may be required.

Electricity

The current is 240/250 volts and 50 hertz alternating current. Universal outlets for 110 volts shavers and small appliances are usually found in leading hotels and motels. For larger appliances, such as hairdryers, you will need a converter and a special flat three-pin adaptor to fit Australian power outlets.

Departure Tax

A departure tax of A$20 is payable by all travellers. It may be paid at a post office prior to departure or at the airport. Only Australian currency is accepted.

GETTING ACQUAINTED

Geography

Sydney is located on the south-east coast of New South Wales. With its population of around 3.5 million people, it is the oldest, largest and liveliest city in Australia. It spreads over 1,736 square kilometres (670 square miles), considerably larger in area than Rome or Los Angeles County, but the population density is a low 277 people per square kilometre. Sydney is divided by the harbour into north and south. The famous Bridge spans the bay to link these two areas. Places of tourist interest are located on both sides of the harbour; the city centre is on the southern shore.

Arriving by Air

Sydney (Kingsford Smith) Airport is located on Botany Bay, nine kilometres (5.5 miles) from the city centre. There are, in effect, three terminals: the international at the western side of the airport, and the two adjacent domestic terminals of Australian Airlines (from which Compass Airlines also operates) and Ansett Australia (which also houses Eastwest Airlines).

It is essential to arrive with some small bills in a major currency (British pounds, US dollars, Deutschmarks, etc) as you require A$1 to hire a baggage trolley while still in the customs and immigration security area – the currency exchange counter is outside this area. An attendant is on hand in the security area to change your money and issue a trolley.

Government buses operate regularly between the international and domestic terminals (cost A$2). Alternatively, a taxi will cost about A$5. Both can be found at the entrance to any terminal.

There is no rail link between the airport and the city. From all airport terminals you can catch the yellow Airport Express bus (No 300 to the city and 350 to Kings Cross) which costs A$5 and takes about 30 minutes to reach the city and a similar time to Kings Cross.

Both buses go via Central Railway Station. Alternatively, a taxi is faster and will cost about A$15.

Sydney's roads are quite narrow and are very crowded during peak hour traffic. If you are departing from Sydney during the afternoon rush, allow up to an hour to get to the airport.

There are stands at all terminals for all the main rental car companies (Avis, Hertz, Budget, etc). The Travellers Information Service at the far end of the international terminal can supply information and maps of Sydney and assist you to book accommodation.

Arriving by Train

The terminal for all rail journeys into Sydney is Central Railway (known simply as "Central") at the southern end of the city centre. However, nearly all city hotels are outside walking range (particularly if you are carrying baggage) of Central. There is an adjoining electric suburban rail station with regular trains into the city centre and the suburbs, but there are some flights of stairs to be negotiated. A taxi from Central railway to downtown or Kings Cross hotel will cost about A$5. Or there is a bus stop with regular departures to the city and suburbs.

Arriving by Bus

There is an extensive inter-state bus trade and fares are cheaper than rail or air. Most of the bus terminals are on the fringes of the city centre. You will probably require a government city bus or taxi journey to reach your hotel.

Tourist Information Service

A free information service is available on 6695111, 8 am to 6 pm, every day. Advice on accommodation, tours, shopping, almost everything .

Climate

The wettest months are March and June, the coldest is July and the hottest are January and February. Mean temperatures: summer 21.7°C (71°F), autumn 18.1°C (64.6°F), winter 12.6°C (54.7°F), spring 17.4°C (63.3°F).

Time

Sydney is on Australian Eastern Standard Time, 10 hours ahead of Greenwich Mean Time. It is half an hour ahead of Adelaide and Darwin, and two hours ahead of Perth. Daylight saving operates between October and March, when the clocks are advanced one hour to Eastern Summer Time.

On Eastern Standard Time, when it is 12 noon in Sydney it is:

11 am today in Tokyo
10 am today in Hong Kong/
Manila/Singapore
9 am today in Jakarta/Bangkok
3 am today in Paris/Rome/
Frankfurt/Amsterdam
2 am today in London
9 pm yesterday in New York/
Washington, DC
6 pm yesterday in San Francisco/
Los Angeles
4 pm yesterday in Honolulu
(For Eastern Summer Time deduct one hour from the above times.)

Weights and Measures

Australia uses metric measurements. The main conversions are:

1 metre = 3.28 feet
1 kilometre = 0.62 miles
1 kilogram = 2.20 pounds
1 litre = 1.5 pints
(US) = 1.8 pints (UK)
60 kilometres per hour =
37 miles per hour
0 degrees centigrade =
32 degrees Fahrenheit
25 degrees centigrade =
70 degrees Fahrenheit
36.9 degree centigrade =
98.4 degrees Fahrenheit (normal body temperature)

Tipping

Tipping is not obligatory in Australia – it is always your choice. However, a small gratuity for special service is appreciated. Hairdressers and taxi drivers do not expect to be tipped. In restaurants it is usual to tip waiters up to 10 per cent (maximum) of the bill for good service.

Security and Crime

Sydney is a relatively safe city, in which you do not need to worry unduly about mugging or theft. However, take the usual security precautions and don't tempt thieves. Avoid dark, empty lanes late at night in the city, don't leave your hotel room unlocked or money, camera etc unattended, and keep wallets and purses out of sight.

GETTING AROUND

Taxis

You can stop and hire a taxi wherever you see an empty one. Initial hiring fee is A$1.70 and A$0.90 kilometre thereafter. Phone bookings cost A$1 extra. Smoking is not permitted in public vehicles, so ask your taxi driver first before you light up. Make sure the driver knows how to get to your destination if it's a small street in an obscure suburb. If you have a complaint, take note of the driver's name – every driver has to display a photo and identity card – and cab number, then call the taxi company.

The main taxi companies serving the

inner city are:

Premier Taxis: 8974000
Taxis Combined Services: 3328888
Legion Cabs: 2899000
RSL Taxis: 6990144

In addition, there are two companies that operate water taxis on the harbour (which cost much more than road cabs):

Aqua Cabs: 9290477
Taxis Afloat: 9224252

Urban Trains, Buses and Ferries

The Urban Transit Authority publishes a map which shows Sydney's train, bus and ferry services. It costs A$1 and is available from news agents or from the Urban Transit Authority Travel & Tours Centre, 11–13 York Street, Sydney, where you can also pick up free timetables.

Trains

Sydney is serviced by an extensive network of electric trains and these are by far the quickest way to get around. The service is frequent, and all services can be joined on the City Circle underground system. Smoking is not allowed.

Buses

Extensive bus services are run mostly by the State Transit Authority, with main bus terminuses at Circular Quay, Wynyard Square and at the Central Railway Station.

A free city bus service, number 777, operates from York Street on a loop around the Domain and back. Another free bus route, **666**, runs between Wynyard Station and the Art Gallery every 30 minutes, daily.

Distinctive red government buses known as **Sydney Explorers** roam through a terrific 20 kilometres of Sydney city sights, and will let you off at any of 22 stops to rejoin them at any time later. In addition, your A$12 ticket (special fares for families, etc) allows you to ride free on all other city buses throughout the same day. The Sydney

Explorer leaves at 17-minute intervals from Circular Quay, from 9.30 am to 5 pm daily. The complete round trip takes about 90 minutes. Purchase tickets from the Travel Centre of New South Wales (19 Castlereagh Street, tel: 231444), or on board the bus.

Day Rover tickets entitle holders to unlimited travel on any suburban bus, train or ferry for A$7. Obtain more information on these and other deals from the State Transit Authority Travel & Tours Centre 11–13 York Street, or ring Metro. Trips on 954 4422.

Ferries and Cruises

The ferries are by far the nicest way of getting around Sydney. They depart from Circular Quay, where the Urban Transit Authority issues free timetables. The longest regular ferry runs are to Meadowbank and the Manly ferry, which covers 11 kilometres in 35 minutes. The shortest ride is to Kirribilli and offers a panorama of the city skyline within a 10-minute trip.

Services are also available at the Royal National Park to the south and on Pittwater to the north. The NSW Travel Centre has the necessary details. There is a variety of commercial harbour cruises, as well as lunchtime and supper cruises, such as Captain Cook harbour cruises from Circular Quay wharf number six. Departing morning, afternoon and night, they include – along with the scenery and commentary – coffee, lunch or dinner. Adult fares range from A$12 to A$45.

Monorail

A monorail runs between Darling Harbour and the City Flat fare is A$2, and the trains run every five minutes from 9 am to 9 pm.

Tourist Information

Australian Tourist Commission offices provide plenty of advice and brochures for people coming to Australia:

Level 3 80 William Street
Woolloomooloo Sydney 2011

Tel: (02) 3601111, Fax: (02) 3316469, Tlx: 22322

The Travel Centre of New South Wales is located at the MLC Building, 19 Castlereagh Street, near Martin Place. The staff will make rail, coach, air and accommodation bookings for you, as well as provide information and brochures. The Travel Centre is open Monday to Friday 9 am to 5 pm. Tel: 2314444.

Additional information is available by phone from the Travellers Information Service on 6695111, daily from 6 am to 11 pm. The Sydney Convention and Visitors bureau shares a kiosk in Martin Place with "Halftix" (see Nightlife), and is a very useful source of information. Tel: 235-2424. There is also an information booth at the western end of Circular Quay.

WHERE TO STAY

Sydney has a large number of hotels in all categories – with more opening all the time. We have weighted this list very much towards the city and Kings Cross – if you have a particular desire to be in a certain suburb, check with your agent or the Travel Centre of New South Wales – there will probably be accommodation nearby. Hotel laundry services are expensive but there are many laundromats in the near suburbs.

The Travel Centre of New South Wales operates an accommodation booking service – it will find you a place to stay at no charge. Visit the offices at 19 Castlereagh Street, Sydney, or call (02) 2314444. It is open from 9 am to 5 pm Monday to Friday. You can also find and book accommodation at the Travellers Information Centre at the International Terminal at Sydney Airport. It is open from 5 am until after the last flight each day, every day (tel: 02-6691583).

Deluxe

A very well appointed room in one of these establishments can cost upwards from A$250 to about A$400 (single or double) – but much better deals are available if you shop around. Air-conditioning, private bathrooms, TV, direct dial telephones, large beds and minibars are standard in all these properties. Most of them are less than five years old. Breakfast is usually extra, from about A$15 to A$30.

Inter-Continental
117 Macquarie Street Sydney 2000
Tel: (02) 2300200
Soaring out of the shell of the historic colonial-style Treasury Building right in the business district, this new 31-storey, 544-room hotel combines old world style and modern facilities.

Nikko
81 Macleay Street Potts Point 2011
Tel: (02) 3683000
A modern, new (1990) hotel with some excellent restaurants with 472 rooms on 17 storeys, the westward-facing ones having Sydney's best views of the city skyline. This is a more relaxed area than adjoining King's Cross.

Park Hyatt
7 Hickson Street The Rocks
Sydney 2000
Tel: (02) 2411234
Perfect location on Sydney Cove for this new (1990) hotel. 163 rooms on four storeys, pool, spa, sauna and incredible views keep this hotel near-full year round.

Parkroyal at Darling Harbour
150 Day Street Sydney 2000
Tel: (02) 2614444
Opened in the second half of 1991 overlooking Darling Harbour, this 295-room hotel over 10 levels takes full advantage of the newly developed part of town. It's only a short walk to the city.

Ramada Renaissance
30 Pitt Street Sydney 2000
Tel: (02) 2597000
The flagship for Ramada in the South Pacific opened in the business heart of Sydney in 1989. There are 630 rooms on 32 storeys, and four floors are for Ramada executive club guests.

Regent Sydney
199 George Street Sydney 2000
Tel: (02) 2380000
Has been Sydney's best hotel for most of the past decade. Good location at Circular Quay and impressive atrium foyer. 620 rooms on 36 floors.

Ritz-Carlton
93 Macquarie Street
Tel: (02) 2524600
Grand in American classical manner furnished in antiques and permanently burning open fires. A boutique-style with 119 rooms on 10 floors that opened in 1990.

Sebel Town House
23 Elizabeth Bay Road
Elizabeth Bay 2011
Tel: (02) 3583244
The facade is unimpressive and the location is out-of-the-way but the Sebel, which first opened in 1963, has long been the address for visiting celebrities. The 193 rooms are excellent – service unobtrusive and exemplary.

Sheraton Wentworth
61–101 Phillip Street Sydney 2000
Tel: (02) 2300700
For more than 22 years, an enduring part of Sydney's five-star hospitality scene. 465 rooms on 17 floors, frequented by regulars who appreciate relaxed attentive service.

Expensive

Priced at about A\$150 to A\$200 per room (double or single) these hotels rate from three to four-and-a-half stars. All have direct dial telephones, air conditioning, TV/radio and en suite bathrooms.

Chateau Sydney
14 Macleay Street
Potts Point 2011
Tel: (02) 358 2500
In the centre of Kings Cross, this hotel has 96 rooms, a heated pool, barbecue and laundry.

Hilton International
Sydney Airport 20 Levey Street
Arncliffe 2205
Tel: (02) 5970122
This 270-room hotel (over nine floors) is out of the way for the city but very convenient to the international terminal. Its relatively cheap price relates more to its location than any lack of amenities: there is a pool, tennis, squash – and a golf course next door.

Resort Hotel Central Plaza
Corner of George and Quay Streets
Sydney 2000
Tel: (02) 2122544
Down towards Darling Harbour, this 120-room property has a pool, spa, sauna, restaurant and shopping arcade.

Sheraton Sydney Airport
Corner of O'Riordan and Robey Streets
Mascot 2020
Tel: (02) 2351277
Open in April 1991, this 318-room hotel has double glazing and in-house videos for those wanting a rest, a heated pool and fitness centre for those who don't.

York

5 York Street Sydney 2000
Tel: (02) 2647747
Very close to the Harbour Bridge, this
property consists of 130 self-contained
apartments. It has a heated pool, spa,
sauna and laundry.

Moderate

Priced at about A$100 to A$150 per
room (double or single) these hotels are
comfortable and clean without being
plush.

Kendall

122 Victoria Street
Potts Point 2011
Tel: (02) 3573200
Boutique private hotel of 22 rooms, all
with en suites, TV, direct dial phones and
a pleasant conservatory full of plants as
breakfast venue.

Park Regis

Corner of Castlereagh and
Park Streets Sydney 2000
Tel: (02) 2676511
Situated in the centre of Sydney's
shopping district, near the Town Hall, this
air-conditioned 120-room hotel provides
TV, radio, direct dial phones and
refrigerator.

Russell

143A George Street Sydney 2000
Tel: (02) 2413543
A two-storey boutique private hotel in
The Rocks area of Sydney, this has 30
rooms, some with showers, some with TV,
all with heating and fans, radio and direct
dial telephones. Tariff includes a large
continental breakfast.

Westbury

221 Darlinghurst Road
Darlinghurst 2010
Tel: (02) 3603222
Well furnished air-conditioned small
hotel of 67 rooms in the heart of
Darlinghurst with restaurant, rooftop pool
and sauna. Each room has en suites, TV,
direct dial phones and mini bar.

Hostels

Sydney has three city hostels operated
by the Youth Hostel Association. The
one at 262–264 Glebe Point Road, tel:
6928414, has 120 beds. The second, at
28 Ross Street, Forest Lodge, tel:
6920747, is a small hostel of only 32
beds. The third, with 250 beds and a
rooftop swimming pool, is at 51
Hereford Street, Glebe, tel: 6605577.
Hostel charge is from A$14 per night.

There is a YWCA in the heart of
Sydney – at 5 Wentworth Avenue,
Darlinghurst, tel: 2642451. It has 100
beds. Single shared starts at A$30,
private A$52. Twin shared is A$50 and
private A$65.

There are many privately run hostels in
the Kings Cross area, particularly in
Victoria Street. The Down Under Hostel,
25 Hughes Street, Kings Cross, tel:
3581143, is well-run and good value, but
occasionally gets overcrowded. The
reception area has a notice board that
offers items for sale, and useful tourist
tips. The Kings Cross Back Packers
Hostel, 165 Victoria Street, tel: 3563232,
has 78 beds.

Budget hotels are mainly located in the
city, Kings Cross or Bondi. In the city is
the Sydney Tourist Hotel at 40 Pitt
Street, tel: 2115777. Directly opposite is
the CB Private Hotel, tel: 2115115, with
200 rooms. In Kings Cross, the Gala

Private Hotel at 23 Hughes Street, tel: 356-3406, and Springfield Lodge at 9 Springfield Avenue, tel: 3583222, are worth a look.

Business Hours and Public Holidays

Sydney retail trading hours are generally 9 am to 5.30 pm, Monday to Friday, and 9 am to 4 pm on Saturday. Thursday night is late-night shopping, until 9 pm. Restaurants, snack bars, bookshops and local corner stores are open till late in the evening and sometimes all weekend. Most businesses are closed on Saturday and Sunday. Banks are open from 9.30 am to 4 pm Monday to Thursday, and until 5 pm on Friday.

The Kings Cross branch of Thomas Cook is open from 8.45 am to 5.30 pm, Monday to Friday, and from 8.45 am to 1 pm at weekends.

All banks, post offices, government and private offices and most shops close on public holidays, which are as follows:

New Year's Day (1 January)
Australia Day (26 January)
Good Friday
Easter Saturday
Easter Monday
ANZAC Day (25 April)
Queen's Birthday (2nd Monday in June)
Bank Holiday (1st Monday in August)
Labour Day (1st Monday in October)
Christmas Day (25 December)
Boxing Day (26 December)

HEALTH AND EMERGENCIES

In an emergency requiring police assistance or ambulance service, or in the case of fire, dial 000. Other emergency numbers: Crisis Centre 358-6577, Rape Crisis Centre 8196565, Interpreter Service 221111.

Medical

Hospitals and doctors are readily available, but overseas visitors are not covered by free government Medicare. A visit to the doctor will cost A$30 and up. British passport holders are eligible for free basic emergency care at public hospitals, via a reciprocal agreement. A travellers' health and accident insurance policy is recommended.

Pharmacies

"Chemists" or pharmacies have qualified professionals who dispense prescribed medication. They also also carry familiar brands of general medications, cosmetics, toiletries, etc. Visitors are allowed to bring up to four week's supply of prescribed medications. For larger quantities, keep a doctor's certificate to avoid difficulties at Customs. There are a number of late-night pharmacies in the inner city area, most located around Kings Cross:

Belgenny Pharmacobert, Bourke Street, Darlinghurst, tel: 3604959

Crest Hotel Pharmacy, 111 Darlinghurst Road, Kings Cross, tel: 3581822

Crown Street Pharmacy, 672 Crown Street, Surry Hills, tel: 69 7259

Dental

For dental emergencies, call 6920333 or 6920598, or consult the Dentists section in the yellow pages.

Drinking Water

It is safe to drink tap water in any Australian town. Bottled mineral water is also available everywhere.

Sunburn

The summer sun in Sydney is extremely strong. Wear a wide-brimmed hat to protect your face and avoid sunbathing between 10.30 am and 3.30 pm. Sunscreens are readily available.

COMMUNICATIONS AND NEWS

Australia Post Offices are open 9 am–5 pm on business days, and Sydney's General Post Office (in Martin Place) is also open Saturday mornings between 8.30 am and noon. Post offices will hold mail for visitors, as will American Express offices for their members.

Telephone and Fax

Public telephones are widespread throughout Sydney. Local calls from them cost 30 cents for an unlimited time. STD (Subscriber Trunk Dialling) is for calling long distance within Australia. STD calls are cheapest between 10 pm and 8 am. Credit card phones are also available.

ISD (International Subscriber Dialling) is used for direct dialling overseas. ISD public phones are fairly common at post offices, airports and hotel foyers.

If you are staying at an international hotel you should be able to request the services of their fax for both incoming and outgoing messages: otherwise faxes can be sent from post offices.

Newspapers and Magazines

Sydney has two daily newspapers, the *Sydney Morning Herald* and the multi-edition *Telegraph Mirror*. The *Financial Review* and *The Australian* are national dailies. The *Sydney Morning Herald* is a must on Fridays when its green "Metro" entertainment guide is included. Sundays are for the tabloids with the *Sun-Herald* and the *Sunday Telegraph*.

The Bulletin is a weekly magazine which includes the Australian edition of *Newsweek*. The *Guardian Weekly* is on sale at most newsagents. Airmail copies of overseas newspapers and journals are available at specialised outlets, such as in Kings Cross or Martin Place.

HELPFUL INFORMATION

Sports Facilities

Sailing: The yachting season runs from Sept to May. Races and regattas are held nearly every weekend.

Golf: There are many public courses for the visiting golfer. Check the yellow pages, then call the course club house for details.

Running and Jogging: Centennial Park, the Domain and Bondi Beach are popular spots for running or jogging.

Skiing: The ski season is between June and September in the Snowy Mountains, to the south-west of Sydney. Crowded slopes, fair snow and expensive accommodation.

Tennis: Sydney has numerous public courts and private tennis clubs. Look in the yellow pages and call the club for details.

In addition there are hockey, ice-skating and roller-skating rinks, gliding clubs, squash courts and more. Ask at the NSW Travel Centre for more details.

Horse Racing: Sydney has six race tracks. Randwick is the closest; races are scheduled throughout the year at Canterbury, Rosehill and Warwick Farm. Trotting races are held Friday nights at Harold Park, and greyhound races on Saturday nights at Harold Park or Wentworth Park.

Rugby League: Games are played from March to September at the Sydney Sports Ground and at many suburban ovals.

Cricket: The season runs from October to March and international and interstate matches are spread throughout this period. Games are played at the Sydney Cricket Ground as well as suburban ovals.

Motor Racing: Eastern Creek raceway has regular car and motorcycle meetings throughout the year.

Surf Carnivals: Held at one of Sydney's ocean beaches on most Saturdays between October and March. The carnivals consist of swimming, surfboat and board-paddling events.

Surfboard Riding: In summer and

autumn there are surfboard competitions. Listen for the morning radio surf reports on MMM-FM and JJJ-FM.

Yacht Races: Held every Saturday. The spectators' ferry leaves Circular Quay at 2 pm. The start of the Sydney-to-Hobart Yacht Race on Boxing Day is a major event in Sydney's sporting calendar.

Aerobics: Dozens of gyms, such as Healthlands, Fitness Network, City Gym, offer many classes each day.

Sydney for the Disabled

Advance notice with relevant details of your disability will ensure the best assistance from the airline, hotel or railway office. The NSW Travel Centre publication, *Sydney Visitor's Guide*, details all the places that it recommends to disabled visitors. Cinemas and restaurants are happy to assist, although not all cater for wheelchairs. Specially outfitted taxis are available, but must be booked in advance. Tel: 3390200. The Australian Council for the Rehabilitation of the Disabled (ACROD) can be contacted on 8094484.

USEFUL ADDRESSES

Airline Offices

Aerolineas Argentinas
Level 2 580 George Street
Sydney 2000
Tel: 2833660

Air Caledonie International
Level 10 403 George Street
Sydney 2000
Tel: 2678455

Air Nauru
Ground Floor 72 Pitt Nauru
Sydney 2000
Tel: 2324909

Air New Zealand
7th floor 90 Arthur Street
North Sydney 2061
Tel: 9654111

Air Nuigini
100 Clarence Street Sydney
Tel: 2323100

Air Pacific
105 Pitt Street Sydney 2000
Tel: (008) 230150, 9570150

Alitalia
2nd Floor 32 Bridge Street
Sydney 2000
Tel: 271308, 277836, 279 133

All Nippon Airlines
Level 1 301 George Street
Sydney 2000
Tel: 2622855, 2622888

American Airlines
First Floor 221 Miller Street
North Sydney 2060
Tel: 9542764

British Airways
Suite 4201 MLC Centre
19–29 Martin Place Sydney 2000
Tel: 2321777

Canadian Airlines International
1st Floor 30 Clarence Street
Sydney 2000
Tel: (008) 251321, 297843

Cathay Pacific Airways
28 O'Connell Street Sydney 2000
Tel: 2312222

Continental Airlines
13th Floor 83 Clarence Street
Sydney 2000
Tel: 2328222

Garuda Indonesian Airways
175 Clarence Street Sydney 2000
Tel: 2322211

JAT Yugoslav Airlines
126–130 Phillip Street Sydney 2000
Tel: 2212199

Japan Airlines
Norwich House 19 Bligh Street
Sydney 200000
Tel: 2369911

KLM Royal Dutch Airlines
5 Elizabeth Street Sydney 2000
Tel: 2316333

Lufthansa
143 Macquarie Street Sydney 2000
Tel: 275334

Malaysian Airlines
American Express Tower
388 George Street Sydney 2000
Tel: 2323377, 2315066

Northwest Airlines
309 Kent Street Sydney 2000
Tel: 2904455

Olympic Airways
44 Pitt Street Sydney 2000
Tel: 2512044

Philippine Airlines
49 York Street Sydney 2000
Tel: 298475

Polynesian Airlines
50 King Street Sydney 2000
Tel: 2681431

Qantas Airways
Qantas House International Centre
George Street Sydney 2000
Tel: 9570111

Singapore Airlines
Singapore Airlines House
17–19 Bridge Street Sydney 2000
Tel: 2360111

Thai International
75–77 Pitt Street Sydney 2000
Tel: 2511722

United Airlines
10 Barrack Street Sydney 2000
Tel: 2331111

UTA French Airlines
33–35 Bligh Street Sydney 2000
Tel: 2213911

FURTHER READING

General
Australian Dreaming: 40,000 Years of Aboriginal History. Edited by Jennifer Isaacs. Lansdowne Press, Sydney, 1980

Borthwick, John and David McGonigal, *Cityguide: Sydney* and *Insight Guide: Australia*. APA Publications, Hong Kong

McGonigal, David, *Wilderness Australia: A Fragile Splendour*. Reed Books, 1990

Morrison, Reg, and Mark Lang, *The Colours of Australia*. Lansdowne Press, Sydney, 1982

Raymond, Robert, *Australia, The Greatest Island*. Lansdowne Press, Sydney, 1982

The Australian Adventure. Australian Adventure Publications, Sydney, 1987

Wilson, Robert, *The Book of Australia*. Lansdowne Press, Sydney, 1982

History
Barnard, Majorie Faith, *A History of Australia*. Angus & Robertson, Sydney, 1962

Blainey, Geoffrey, *A Land Half Won*. Macmillian, Melbourne, 1980

Clark, Charles Manning. *A Short History of Australia*. Macmillan, Melbourne, 1981

Horne, Donald, *The Australian People: Biography of a Nation*. Angus & Robertson, Sydney, 1972

Kepert, L, *History As It Happened*.

Nelson, Melbourne, 1981

Social History
Conquest, R, *Dusty Distances: Yesterday's Australia*. Rigby, Adelaide, 1978
Kepert, L, *History As It Happened*. Nelson, Melbourne, 1981
Young, C, *The New Gold Mountain: The Chinese in Australia*. S A Raphael Arts, Richmond, 1977

Australian Language
The Macquarie Dictionary. Macquarie University, Sydney, 1982
Wilkes, G A, *Dictionary of Australian Colloquialisms*. University Press, Sydney, 1990

ART & PHOTO CREDITS

76, 94	**Stockshots/ Roy Bisson**
11T, 11B, 13, 15, 17, 19B, 20T, 21T, 21B, 22T, 23B, 25, 26, 27T, 27B, 37T, 40T, 40B, 42, 43T, 43B, 47, 49T, 53, 55, 57, 58T, 58B, 59T, 59B, 78, 79, 86, 88, 91, 92B, 96T, 96B, 97, 101B	**John Borthwick**
36T, 45, 52B, 63, 75, 84, 90	**Stockshots/ Geoff Brown**
66, 80B	**Stockshots/ Phill Castleton**
36B, 69, 80T, 83, 87	**Stockshots/ Myke Gerrish**
4, 20B, 50B, 89,	**Stockshots/ Graeme Goldin**
51	**Stockshots/ M. Hall**
10T, 14, 19T, 22B, 30B, 31T, 31B, 35T, 35B, 39, 73, 101T	**David McGonigal**
cover, 29, 32, 44, 61T, 65B, 72, 74, 81	**Stockshots/ Graham Monro**
92T	**Stockshots/ Paul Nevin**
38, 67	**Stockshots/ Peter J. Robinson**
61B, 82	**Stockshots/ Loreli Simmonds**
1	**Paul Steel**
46, 65T, 77	**Stockshots**
10B, 71	**Stockshots/ North Sullivan**
12, 30T, 33, 48T, 54, 68, 98	**Stockshots/ Clifford White**
Cover Design	**Klaus Geisler**
Maps	**Berndtson & Berndtson**

NOTES